The Personal Vision Workbook

The Personal Vision Workbook

The revolutionary process that shows you how to explore your identity, passion, and core values ... and turn them into a compelling personal vision for your life

PHYSICAL

SPIRITUAL

EMOTION

JOURNEY

CULTURAL

COGNITIVE

Tobin Burgess
Kevin Pugh
Leo Sevigny

THOMSON
DELMAR LEARNING

Australia   Brazil   Canada   Mexico   Singapore   Spain   United Kingdom   United States

The Personal Vision Workbook

Tobin Burgess, Kevin Pugh, and Leo Sevigny

Vice President, Career Education SBU:
Dawn Gerrain

Director of Learning Solutions:
Sherry Dickinson

Managing Editor:
Robert L. Serenka, Jr.

Acquisitions Editor:
Martine Edwards

Editorial Assistant:
Christina Gifford
Falon Ferraro

Director of Production:
Wendy A. Troeger

Production Manager:
J.P. Henkel

Associate Content Project Manger:
Angela Iula

Director of Marketing:
Wendy E. Mapstone

Channel Manager:
Gerard McAvey

Cover Design:
Suzanne Nelson

Composition:
Interactive Composition Corporation

Library of Congress Cataloging-in-Publication Data

Burgess, Tobin.
   The personal vision workbook / by Tobin Burgess, Kevin Pugh, and Leo Sevigny.
      p. cm.
   ISBN 1-4018-9939-0
   1. Success—Psychological aspects. 2. Self-actualization (Psychology) 3. Visualization. 4. Identification (Psychology)   I. Pugh, Kevin. II. Sevigny, Leo. III. Title.
      BF637.S8B87   2007
      158.1—dc22

                                              2006017560

NOTICE TO THE READER

DEDICATION:

To Sebastien, Whitney, and Garrett

DEDICATION

Contents

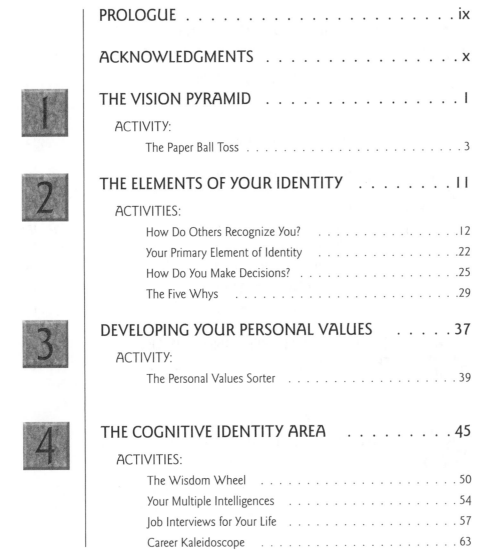

Prologue

Have you ever found yourself at a crossroads in life? Faced with multiple paths for your life to pursue, you may have felt underqualified to make a choice. You may have felt like you were being carried along by a fast-moving current, suspended in a stream of social pressures that relentlessly nudged you forward. There is a better way!

You live in a time where the human spirit lives in jeopardy. Your identity is under constant attack from images in the mass media (Internet, television, movies, radio, and print), judgments from friends and family, and social institutions that prescribe acceptable standards of behavior, thought, emotions, and relationships. The ever-quickening Information Age intensifies the pressures to conform by appealing to our every sense. How do you maintain a clear sense of self, given all the external messages to think, act, and feel in ways that you are not? Identity has become as much the fabrication of society as it is a true reflection of who you are. But you are more than how others define you.

Identity is a sacred part of your being and is worthy of intentional exploration. *The Personal Vision Workbook* is your opportunity to find and embrace who you are. Your spirit and your life essence will guide you best if you deeply understand what they are trying to say to you. So open your ears, open your mind, and prepare yourself for a valuable awakening.

> " I don't want to get to the end of my life and find that I lived just the length of it. I want to have lived the width of it as well."
>
> —*DIANE ACKERMAN*

IDENTITY IS A SACRED PART OF YOUR BEING

AND IS WORTHY OF INTENTIONAL EXPLORATION.

This book is not a "read-me-from-cover-to-cover" kind of experience. It is a thoughtful, careful process of self-discovery in which the most important author is you. No two people will experience this book the same way, just as no two people will live their lives the same way. Focus on the process of understanding your core identity, and the product of personal vision will arrive on its own. This is the key to you *being you*!

Acknowledgments

It is a true honor to acknowledge the people who supported us in the creation of this book. While our names may be on the cover, it is the mentoring, friendship, and love from the following people that really helped us to flesh out our ideas into activities, activities into workshops, and workshops into a complete book. We wish to call out and personally thank just a few of these individuals and groups.

First and foremost we must acknowledge the unending support we received from our families and loved ones. This book would not have turned out like it did without the love, encouragement, support, and ideas of Bethany Pugh and Heather Sevigny. Thank you for believing in us. We also must thank our parents, Ron and Lynne Pugh, Ghislaine and Ron Girouard, Richard and Venise Sevigny, and Chris and Scott Burgess. Each raised us to believe in ourselves, and in the power of possibilities and dreams, especially when paired with vision.

Thank you to the students, faculty, and staff from Syracuse University, Sonoma State University, Katharine Gibbs Schools, Baldwin-Wallace College, SUNY New Paltz, The University of Illinois Urbana–Champaign, the Community College of Vermont, the University of Colorado at Boulder, and Lyndon State College for allowing us to "test-drive" the concepts and activities presented in this book. If not for the fertile minds and empowerment of these institutions, this book would not be what it is.

Finally, thanks to the many who took the time to review and provide meaningful feedback, especially Trent Norman, Lori Lander, Anthea Johnson, Regina Tirella, Chris Schmidt, Christy Cerrone, Karin Anderson, Jessie Sell, Karen Alonge, Annemarie Vaccaro-Phillips, Mo Phillips, Mike Murphy, Tera Porterfield, Cyndie Morozumie, Chuck Rhodes, Scott Peska, Michael and Sarah Knox, Robin Berkowitz-Smith, Bryan and Stacey Scanlon, Tom Buckles, Sarah Englehardt, Dan Bauer, the late Jeff Moss, and all of the staff at Thomson Delmar Learning.

The Vision Pyramid

THE GREATEST DISCOVERY OF MY GENERATION IS THAT A HUMAN

BEING CAN ALTER LIFE BY ALTERING ATTITUDES OF THE MIND.

■

—WILLIAM JAMES

WELCOME TO
THE PERSONAL VISION WORKBOOK!

You are about discover a new you. You will discover a "you" that is in harmony with the multiple facets of your life. This focused and clear "you" will stand up to the greatest of pressures with a clear sense of purpose. The visioning process in these pages is designed to assist you in finding answers to your life's most pressing questions. You will align your life around your core values and then will create tangible goals directed toward a clear vision. In this workbook, you will learn more about yourself than you have ever known before.

IN THIS WORKBOOK, YOU WILL LEARN MORE ABOUT YOURSELF

THAN YOU HAVE EVER KNOWN BEFORE.

Do you ever find your life in conflict or at odds? For example, have you found that who you are at home with family and friends is different than who you are at work or school? Do you ever feel like the decisions you make in one aspect of your life come at the expense of another aspect? A decision to accept a new job may come at the expense of time to build and maintain important relationships in your life. For example, time spent focusing on your spiritual awareness may come at the expense of day-to-day demands. You are not alone.

These feelings of imbalance and opposition are very common and, at different points, they impact everyone. American culture often focuses attention on one aspect of life, such as fitness, academics, career, or spirituality, without considering the effects on other aspects of life. Think of the late night infomercial that promises that if you strengthen one area of your life, everything will get better. The miracle diet, the super efficient workout, a correspondence course, or some other miracle product in pill form seldom impacts more than a very minute part of you . . . but so much more is promised! Even things that are more tangible, like a promotion, a new relationship, or even a spiritual awakening—taken alone—rarely solve all of life's problems. Focusing too much on one aspect of your life will lead to imbalance with other life demands. It is finding personal balance in all areas of your personal journey that will give you the most satisfying life possible.

Consider, for example, the story of former President Bill Clinton. In his autobiography, *My Life,* Clinton describes the "parallel lives" he led throughout his youth that culminated in his rise to the presidency and intimate affair with Monica Lewinsky. His energy and passion for politics led him to one of the most powerful positions in the world. However, his personal life was in crisis, which culminated in indiscretions that nearly cost him the presidency. The success in one area of his life, politics, could not overcome the indiscretions in his personal life, infidelity. Of course, this is a very public and extreme example, but we all have experienced imbalance at some point in our lives. How often have you found yourself living a life where one part of you is in active conflict with another?

> Society, my dear, is like salt water, good to swim in but hard to swallow."
>
> —*ARTHUR STRINGER, "THE SILVER POPPY"*

VISIONING IS A POWERFUL TOOL

Close your eyes for a moment. Now picture your life in balance. Picture your life with clear purpose, meaning, and direction. Picture what it would be like to know who you really are regardless of any of life's challenges. Imagine a personal journey where every turn you take and every decision you consider is made from your core being. You've begun the process of visioning. The picture may not be totally clear right now, but you have begun the process. Creating personal vision is a powerful tool that will help you to reach your fullest potential.

Visioning has transcended history in various forms to help countless people find purpose, answers, and direction in their lives. Engaging in this process, you will follow in the footsteps of these traditions using a fresh, hands-on, and interactive approach. Be ready to experience parts of you that you may not have known existed.

ENGAGING IN THIS PROCESS, YOU WILL FOLLOW IN THE FOOTSTEPS OF THESE

TRADITIONS USING A FRESH, HANDS-ON, AND INTERACTIVE APPROACH.

The peoples of our world community practice visioning in many forms. The American Indian Lakota tribe has a tradition called the Vision Quest where individuals retreat into nature to listen and watch for a vision that will guide their lives. Athletes, musicians, and artists commonly use visualization by mentally rehearsing their movements prior to performance. Visualization centers the body and mind to enhance performance. Even in the process of childbirth, women are often encouraged to visualize the birth of their child, practice relaxation breathing techniques, and visualize the miraculous conclusion of their labor.

Faiths as diverse as Christianity, Islam, Buddhism, Hindu, Taoism, and Wicca use various forms of meditation, prayer, ritual, and ceremony to channel their energies toward internal clarity and purpose. Businesses and organizations often plan elaborate retreats for groups of people to come together to establish clear organizational vision and mission statements. Each of these approaches to creating vision shares a common theme; they focus on awareness, core values, and developing a sense of clear purpose. Each approach, in its own unique way, channels the energy of the group or individual toward common understanding.

> " Prepare yourself for the world, as the athletes used to do for their exercise; oil your mind and your manners, to give them the necessary suppleness and flexibility; strength alone will not do."
>
> —*EARL OF CHESTERFIELD*

VISION IN ACTION—VISUALIZATION

You can test the power of visioning right where you are sitting with a few pieces of scrap paper, a wastepaper basket (or container), and 8 feet of space. As mentioned before, athletes use visualization routinely to perfect their performances. It is as common to athletes as mission and vision statements are to businesses. Athletes concentrate on mentally rehearsing every aspect of upcoming athletic challenges. They align their conscious and subconscious minds to peak performance. Results are unprecedented . . . and easy to demonstrate.

activity   THE PAPER BALL TOSS

To illustrate the power of visualization, try this simple test for yourself. This exercise will require you to have six sheets of paper that you can crumple up, a wastepaper basket, and 8 feet of space. If you are the perfectionist type, resist the initial urge to perfect and analyze the directions up front. Just wing it!

ACTIVITY PURPOSE

This activity will demonstrate the power of visualization and its ability to help you yield immediate results. ◼

THE STEP BY STEP

1. Crumple up six pieces of paper . . . any 8-½ × 11-inch paper will work.

2. Place a wastepaper basket approximately 6 to 8 feet away.

3. Back up, and without a lot of thought or planning, toss the paper balls into the basket. Complete this step before you read on!

4. Retrieve the paper balls and return to your original tossing spot. Note how successful you were.

5. Now close your eyes, relax, and carefully visualize the perfect toss. Don't rush. Visualize the exact movement of your arm, your breathing pattern, the kind of finger positioning you will need, eye contact with the basket, and so forth. Visualize the

ball leaving your fingers and perfectly floating directly into the basket. This should take 2 to 3 minutes. When you feel you have visualized success, move to the next step.

6 Using this vision, toss the balls into the basket.

7 Compare the results from your first attempts to the results following your visualization.

Reflections

Use the personal space below to answer the following questions:

Why do you think your throws were closer to the basket after visualizing the perfect toss?

In what ways were you able to sense that both your conscious and self conscious mind were working together to align the ball with the basket?

Personal Space

This is your opportunity to add your own thoughts and make notes.

_____

_____

_____

_____

_____

_____

_____

_____

_____

_____

You just utilized visualization to improve a fairly basic skill. Imagine what you could do if you could align your entire life around one consistent vision based on your deepest core values. That is what this experience—the journey that is visioning—is all about! Take a moment to reflect on the potential of creating your own personal vision. Think of how it will impact your ability to focus and improve your life.

THE VISION PYRAMID

The Vision Pyramid shown in Figure 1–1 is a pictorial model for how to create personal vision. Each layer of the pyramid is a progressive step toward creating a deeper understanding of you. The pyramid shape is relevant because it symbolically represents the power to focus energy. Egyptian culture and

FIGURE 1–1
The Vision Pyramid

history give strong examples of the fascination with and symbolic use of pyramids to entomb and preserve the dead.

The geometric shape of a pyramid is hypothesized to channel energy in such a way that it changes the chemical composition of materials placed within it. More recently, this idea was tested and patented by a Czech engineer, Karel Drabl. He used pyramids to actually focus energies to sharpen edges. You will test the power of the Vision Pyramid to focus your energies and help you discover and preserve your true identity.

PERSONAL VISION PYRAMID

The entire Vision Pyramid is based on your core beliefs and values. Each layer of a pyramid depends on the foundation of the previous layer. This hierarchical relationship represents dependency, priority, and importance. Values form the foundation of developing personal goals and so on. By moving up the Vision Pyramid, you will create a base that supports your personal vision. This vision will give you guidance when answering life's tough questions.

The visioning process begins at the base of the pyramid where you will spend the most time exploring the elements of your identity. In this stage you will focus on what makes you unique. Your identity is essentially the composition of the unique characteristics that make you special. By exploring your identity, you will unravel the definitions, judgments, and pressures from others to create your own accurate self-perceptions.

YOUR IDENTITY IS ESSENTIALLY THE COMPOSITION OF THE UNIQUE

CHARACTERISTICS THAT MAKE YOU SPECIAL.

The second level of the Vision Pyramid focuses on the exploration and the application of your core values. Values are personal beliefs that help you to determine what is right, just, and good in the world. They form the foundation from which you choose your actions and evaluate others.

VALUES ARE PERSONAL BELIEFS THAT HELP YOU TO DETERMINE

WHAT IS RIGHT, JUST, AND GOOD IN THE WORLD.

In the next step of the visioning process, you will bridge the gap between your values and actions by establishing personal goals. Personal goals help you to define the specific actions needed to move you toward your ideal life. You determine these goals by identifying the gaps that separate who you are now from who you wish to be. The more specific, measurable, realistic, and timely you make your goals, the better the opportunity you will have to create positive change in your life. In this step you will determine how to actively *live* your values.

THE MORE SPECIFIC, MEASURABLE, REALISTIC, AND TIMELY YOU MAKE

YOUR GOALS, THE BETTER THE OPPORTUNITY YOU WILL HAVE

TO CREATE POSITIVE CHANGE IN YOUR LIFE.

Mission statements provide a synopsis of the strategy behind a set of individual goals. Essentially they are a short, written description of your purpose and direction. Mission statements are easy to remember and clarify where you want to go in life. Many organizations use mission statements to organize, motivate, and direct their employees. Organizational missions make meaning of competing priorities by spelling out the common purpose and strategy of everyone in the organization. The same concept can be applied to your life by creating mission statements that simplify and direct your competing priorities. Personal mission statements summarize a group of personal goals into one strategy.

MISSION STATEMENTS ARE EASY TO REMEMBER AND CLARIFY

WHERE YOU WANT TO GO IN LIFE.

Finally, a personal vision is a powerful symbolic representation of who you want to be. Visions capture the meaning behind all of your mission statements. Visions come in a million different forms. You may find that you wish to capture your vision in words, pictures, music, or symbols. Regardless of the format, your vision will become essential to your personal identity and will be the foundation for future decisions that you make.

YOUR VISION WILL BECOME ESSENTIAL TO YOUR PERSONAL IDENTITY AND

WILL BE THE FOUNDATION FOR DECISIONS THAT YOU MAKE.

PLANNING YOUR TIME

The bulk of your time in this workbook will be focused on self-discovery and exploration of the five primary elements of your identity. You will explore who you are and unravel the labels, stereotypes, and judgments that others give to you. Your renewed identity will then build the foundation for your core values. Once you've found internal consensus around your core values, you will begin to apply them to your daily life. Being honest and open about what aspects of your life need to be changed leads you to personal goals. Personal goals establish specific actions needed to propel your life in positive directions.

Mission statements will then help to summarize your personal goals into direction for your life. Think of a mission statement as a quick and simple synopsis of the active goals in your life. Finally, you will discover that a personal vision becomes self-evident. A personal vision is a picture/feeling/belief of who you want to be. By the time you get to your personal vision, it may occur to you that this is what you were working toward the entire time.

This is not an overnight process; it is a journey! You will change throughout life, and the different parts of your identity will adjust to those changes. This adjustment requires renewed evaluation of core values, mission, and vision. Do not become discouraged; even if you are only able to touch on a few identity areas and experience a selection of the activities within the book, you will gain useful insight about who you are.

If you are completing the *Personal Vision Workbook* as a staff development or classroom exercise, your manager or instructor will provide the proper direction and time frames to help shape your experience. Creating a personal vision is a truly powerful process when you are doing so with a team or group of people who are willing to share their moments of discovery. It is equally powerful to share your enlightenment with others. If you are completing the workbook with your significant other, the understanding that you gain will impact the relationship that you build together. When it comes to creating your personal vision, sharing the journey is a powerful way to make the process feel more real.

> " We lift ourselves by our thought; we climb upon our vision of ourselves. If you want to enlarge your life, you must first enlarge your thought of it and of yourself. Hold the ideal of yourself as you long to be, always, everywhere—your ideal of what you long to attain—the ideal of health, efficiency, success."
>
> —*ORISON SWETT MARDEN*

GOALS, MISSION, AND VISION

Your goals, mission statement, and vision all share one thing in common—they provide direction. Goals, in this context, are specific actions/objectives that, when completed, move you toward accomplishing a mission. Personal goals identify specific activities or behaviors that will help you accomplish life through the guidance of your values. Your personal goals will come from your reflections on the activities within this workbook as well as from other life experiences. To be useful, goals need to be measurable, realistic, and attainable.

To help in understanding the connection among goals, mission statements, and personal vision, observe the continuum shown in Figure 1–2.

Goals are concrete, specific, and measurable actions. They are rooted in reality and have an actual start and end point. If created in a clear format, it is easy to track the progress and outcomes of your goals. They tend to change constantly, because as soon as you reach one goal, you will create another. In other words, you will adjust your goals to meet your changing needs.

FIGURE 1–2
Goal, Mission, Vision Continuum

Here are some elements to consider when creating effective goals:

- Make your goals measurable.

- Create a time-line for each of your goals.

- Make sure your goals are realistic and attainable.

- Find a friend or colleague to help monitor your progress.

On the other side of the continuum, personal vision is much more abstract and represents your life philosophy. A personal vision is who you want to be. It is a life philosophy that does not have a defined start and stop time. In fact, the impact of who you are can transcend many generations as it did for the personal visions of Gandhi, Aristotle, Einstein, and da Vinci. Visions are more about the *way* you live your life than about what you *do* in life. When surroundings change, your personal vision does not change with the surroundings, even if your goals and mission do. Visions are relatively constant over time, especially when compared to goals. Visions should hold up to the test of time, resist social pressures, and be impermeable to judgments by others. Your personal vision is what guides you on your personal life journey.

VISIONS SHOULD HOLD UP TO THE TEST OF TIME, RESIST SOCIAL PRESSURES,

AND BE IMPERMEABLE TO JUDGMENTS BY OTHERS.

Mission statements tend to fall in the middle of this continuum. They change from time to time when circumstances change. Just as large corporations periodically review their business strategy and develop new initiatives, personal mission statements evolve as well.

For example, if a portion of your personal mission statement says "Provide the best care possible for my pets and family to ensure all are happy," and a pet of yours passes away, you may feel a need to change part of your mission statement. You will most certainly have to change the goals that you have set related to being a provider for your pet. Your overall vision, however, will most likely not be impacted by this event, unless the loss of that pet has a major, life-altering impact. Figure 1–3 summarizes the basics of vision, mission, and goals and introduces the idea of core values.

Reflection

Take a moment to reflect on what you have read in this chapter by reviewing the basics of vision, mission, values, and goals.

What is your definition of vision, mission, values, and goals?

What are three questions that you have about this process that have not yet been answered?

Vision	A personal philosophy; who you want to BE, your calling, your mantra
Mission	A summary/synopsis of personal action; a statement that symbolizes the direction of your life in a given identity area
Goals	Specific ACTIONS/objectives that change with life and are measurable and realistic
Core Values	The values that define who you are and bring together all of the elements of your identity

FIGURE 1–3
Vision, Mission, and Goals Summary

Are you feeling a bit skeptical . . . like this is a little too good to be true? Write down your thoughts!

Personal Space

_____

_____

_____

_____

_____

_____

_____

_____

_____

_____

_____

_____

_____

_____

_____

_____

_____

The Elements of Your Identity

A JOURNEY OF A THOUSAND MILES BEGINS WITH A SINGLE STEP.

■

—LAO TZU

WHAT IS IDENTITY?

Visual identity, personal identity, identity theft, corporate identity, identity fraud, identifying information, identifiers . . . the list of descriptive phrases used to encapsulate identity goes on and on. It is hard to hear these references to identity and not think of some of the negative connotations that come with them. When asked, "What is your identity?" what comes to mind? Do you think of your Social Security number, passport, credit card number, bank account? In this technological age, identity is often boiled down to numbers and papers. Awash with e-mail addresses, instant messages, voice mail, bulk mail, and telemarketers, your "identity" becomes a moldable demographic for others' use. Is this what your identity is about? Realistically, identity has little to do with numbers, statistics, and documents created by large institutions and databases. Your true identity is much more personal. It is who you are and who you want to be.

YOUR TRUE IDENTITY IS MUCH MORE PERSONAL. IT IS WHO YOU ARE

AND WHO YOU WANT TO BE.

Webster's *New Collegiate Dictionary* defines *identity* as "the individual characteristics by which a thing or person is recognized." At first glance, this definition may seem like a good depiction of identity. If you wish to identify someone, you would look for unique characteristics that help you recognize the person you are looking for. "He is the short guy over there." "Remember the woman with the lisp at the ticket counter?" The struggle with this definition of identity is that recognition requires a comparison to a societal norm. Only unique characteristics that are different from others are recognized. What about the characteristics that others don't see or are not so unique? Aren't these characteristics just as important to your identity? How many times have you felt labeled by others based on one unique quality? "Look at that redhead over there." "She's the one with the long nose." Identity based solely on comparison is lacking.

Comparisons between elements of what we perceive to be identity are quite common. For example, if you are tall, it refers to a comparison of your height to the average height of others. Being considered a sensitive and caring person means that you are being compared to others who are not as caring. Allowing yourself to be compared is allowing your identity to be defined by others. Worse yet, as the comparison group changes, so does your identity in the eyes of others. You are smart . . . until someone else comes along who is smarter. You are fun . . . until someone else is comparably more fun. By allowing yourself to be identified in this way, your identity constantly changes as your surroundings change.

Your identity is under constant observation by others who wish to compare themselves to you. Stereotyping, labeling, discrimination, assumption, and overall confusion are all possible by-products of identity comparison. Labels are used to simplify. Labels categorize and lump you in with others who are "like you." The visioning process you are about to begin is not about labels, it is about your personal journey through life, and where you want that journey to take you.

THE ROOT OF YOUR IDENTITY IS FAR BEYOND THE SIMPLE LABELS

AND COMPARISONS OF OTHERS.

The root of your identity is far beyond the simple labels and comparisons of others. It is time to rewrite the definition of who you are and recognize what qualities and values are most important. You will construct this new identity by reflecting on the unique qualities that make you special, not just different. The only judgments you will apply to your identity are those that you create yourself to establish core values. This new identity must be built on the basic cornerstones of how you think, feel, look, believe, and relate to others. These cornerstones represent the foundation for the five elements of identity.

ACTIVITY PURPOSE

This activity will help you to sort out perceptions that others have of you and the impact these have on your personal identity. ■

activity 1   HOW DO OTHERS RECOGNIZE YOU?

Before you begin the self-exploration process, begin by reviewing what other people think of you. Sometimes you have to take out the mental garbage before you can organize your personal house. How do others recognize you? What are the unique characteristics to which others pay most attention? What have been the most important experiences in your personal journey?

THE STEP BY STEP

 In Figure 2–1, write down the external labels that others have given you. Think about the unique characteristics that other people have used to recognize you. It is important that you don't overanalyze in this activity. Let your ideas flow without judging their content. Think about the physical, personality, and cultural characteristics that people notice first. For each personal label, describe the impact that it has on your self-perception. It is important to go beyond physical appearance. What do others think about your personality, interests, passions, faith, and social place?

 Place each personal label in Figure 2–2. Then draw a line to the part of your body that it relates to (if applicable).

PERSONAL LABEL	IMPACT THAT IT HAS HAD ON YOUR SELF-PERCEPTION

FIGURE 2–1
Personal Label List

Reflections

Labeling yourself can be pretty difficult. Remember that this activity is designed to clear up mental space for you to create your own identity, and in order to do so, you need to empty some space that is filled by other assumptions and labels. Use the following questions to assist you in processing what this experience was like:

How does it feel to be labeled and to recognize the impact these labels have on you?

What values are attached to these labels? What emotional response do you have to each of your labels?

What are the purposes of these labels? Who do they want you to be?

FIGURE 2–2 Personal Label Diagram

Personal Space

This is your opportunity to add your own thoughts and make notes.

_____
_____
_____
_____
_____
_____
_____
_____
_____
_____
_____
_____
_____
_____
_____
_____

YOUR PERSONAL VISIONING ADVENTURE!

You are a complex being . . . a combination of countless influences, emotions, physical characteristics, thoughts, and motivations. You must consider all of these characteristics to get a clear picture of who you want to be. This is what the personal vision creation process is all about: self-exploration and discovery. To help you navigate through the complexities of your identity, think of your identity as five basic elements: your mind, relationships, heart, body, and spirit. These are the building blocks that make you unique.

PERSONAL VISION CREATION MODEL

Figure 2–3 is a pictorial representation of how personal vision is created from the elements of your identity: your mind (cognitive identity), relationships (cultural identity), heart (emotional identity), body (physical identity), and spirit (spiritual identity). The remaining element is the journey that you take to develop your identity and vision. The triangles also represent the vision pyramids for each of your identity elements. If you recall from Chapter 1, the visioning process is used for self-exploration of your identity, core values, personal goals, mission, and eventually vision. Applying the Vision Pyramid to each of the elements of your identity leads you to a complete personal vision. The remaining element, journey, is the process that moves you forward. It cannot be stressed enough that the goal of the visioning process is not the final outcome, it is the journey that you will take to get there.

You will first explore each element of your identity in detail, then create core values by which to live, establish specific personal goals on which to work, and finally summarize your goals in mission statements. These mission statements, which are based on the elements of your identity, will focus you on your center or personal vision. Your personal vision provides the clarity that you need

FIGURE 2–3
The Elements of Identity

through making difficult decisions, overcoming self-doubt, avoiding false comparisons, and leveraging your best on a daily basis.

YOUR PERSONAL VISION PROVIDES THE CLARITY THAT YOU NEED THROUGH

MAKING DIFFICULT DECISIONS, OVERCOMING SELF-DOUBT, AVOIDING FALSE

COMPARISONS, AND LEVERAGING YOUR BEST ON A DAILY BASIS.

THE 5 ELEMENTS OF IDENTITY

The Personal Vision Creation Model is based on a basic and ancient approach to understanding identity. Most people are familiar with the idea that nature consists of four basic elements: earth, wind, fire, and water. Similarly, this model focuses on these symbolic elements of identity: mind, relationships, heart, body, and spirit (Figure 2–4). The unique qualities of each and their combinations make up the universe of who you are.

These 5 elements have been studied since the early ages across many cultures and continents. Philosophers such as Hippocrates in 460 B.C., Plato in 360 B.C., and Siddhartha Gautama in 566 B.C. developed some of the earliest theories about the connection among mind, body, heart, and spirit. These theories are now the foundation of much of our current knowledge about how humans operate. Today, philosophers, doctors, psychologists, theologians, and academics are still working to understand the full relationships at work among these elements. The elements are the bedrock of who we are and encompass every aspect of our being.

In the following pages you will be given a brief description of each of the elements of identity. After each description, you will have space to write down the initial personal meaning that each element has for you.

Mind	This element is focused on the brain, how you think and process information.
Relationships	This element is about your personal culture, how you relate to others and with yourself.
Heart	This element is focused on your emotions, empathy, and passion.
Body	This element is connected to your physical appearance, health, wellness, and abilities.
Spirit	This element is about life force, the source of energy or animation in your life.
Journey	This symbol represents the dynamic infinite journey of life formed by the combinations of all of these elements of your identity.

FIGURE 2–4
Symbolic Elements of Identity

MIND: COGNITIVE IDENTITY

COGNITIVE IDENTITY

is your personal perspective of
the achievements, improvements,
and exercise of your mind.

The mind is your source of thoughts, reasoning, knowledge, and wisdom. Everyone processes information differently. Some people prefer to think about big picture ideas; others prefer to work with their hands as they problem solve how things come together. Some people think artistically, others pragmatically. Whether you like to read, explore, chat, construct, analyze, or challenge your mind in other ways, these are all important aspects of your cognitive identity.

Cognitive identity is your personal perspective about the achievements, improvements, and exercise of your mind. This aspect of your identity explores how your mind processes information, what mental challenges interest you the most, and the occupational path that you travel. It is your cognitive identity that motivates discovery as a means to fulfill your curiosity. Think of the books that you like to read, interest areas that you want to research, or new skills that you want to gain. This desire to better understand your world is important because it will help to define your intellectual interests and potential career path.

Reflections

How does cognitive identity connect with who you are? Do you think that this element of identity is vital to who you are or not as important as some of the other elements?

What are some basic personal themes and important descriptions that you can give regarding your own Cognitive identity?

Personal Space

_____

_____

_____

_____

_____

_____

_____

_____

_____

_____

_____

_____

_____

_____

_____

_____

_____

CULTURAL IDENTITY

is your personal perspective of society, culture, and personal relationships.

RELATIONSHIPS: CULTURAL IDENTITY

Your cultural identity is your family history, your relationships, and how you interconnect with others. It is the combination of the genetic framework that you were given and the environmental factors that have shaped who you are. It relates to your preference regarding whom you like to spend your time with and the types of cultural characteristics to which you best relate.

Cultural identity also relates to how you maintain personal relationships; in essence, the people with whom you most strongly connect, whether they are from a familial, ethnic, and racial connection or whether that means the "type" of person. Your cultural identity includes how you compare yourself to the rest of the world, your nationality, your socioeconomic class, and even who you love and why.

Reflections

How does cultural identity connect with who you are? Do you think that this element of identity is vital to who you are or not as important as some of the other elements?

What are some basic personal themes and important descriptions that you can give regarding your own cultural identity?

Personal Space

_____

_____

_____

_____

_____

_____

_____

_____

_____

_____

_____

_____

_____

_____

_____

_____

_____

SPIRIT: SPIRITUAL IDENTITY

Spirit is the animating force or source of vitality, energy, strength, and inner peace within you. Everyone is born with a spirit; it is what gives you life. Some believe it is what guides you through life in the form of ethical, religious, or spiritual beliefs, while others see it as the electrical charge that maintains our nervous systems. Spiritual identity is your personal perspective of your religious, ethical, and/or sacred beliefs.

This book looks at spirituality from four perspectives: religion, beliefs, spirit, and ethics. Religion is a set of beliefs, values, and practices based on the teachings of a spiritual leader. Core beliefs are guiding principles for what your origin, purpose, meaning, and place are in the world. Spirit is the animating force or source of vitality, energy, strength, and inner peace in your life. Ethics are a personal doctrine of what is right, just, and good when relating to others. You may find your spirituality drawn to one or all four perspectives. The importance is for you to connect to your spiritual self and draw from the energy that gives you life.

> **SPIRITUAL IDENTITY**
>
> is your personal perspective of your religious, ethical, and/or sacred beliefs.

Reflections

How does spiritual identity connect with who you are? Do you think that this element of identity is vital to who you are or not as important as some of the other elements?

What are some basic personal themes and important descriptions that you can give regarding your own spiritual identity?

Personal Space

_____

_____

_____

_____

_____

_____

_____

_____

_____

_____

_____

_____

_____

_____

_____

THE JOURNEY

The importance of the journey in the visioning process is vital and is well demonstrated by this workbook. You will undertake a wide variety of different activities and exercises that will challenge you to analyze your past and present. You will be asked to study your personal history as you begin the journey of creating your personal vision. While the journey piece of the visioning diagram is not an actual area of identity, it is a vital element in understanding the importance of noticing important cues through your life.

ACTIVITY PURPOSE

To help you determine the element of identity with which you most initially connect, giving you a starting point in the visioning process. ◼

activity 2 **YOUR PRIMARY ELEMENT OF IDENTITY**

You have a connection to all of the elements of identity, but you may find that there are some that feel like they "connect" to you better. There may be one or two that resonate more, based on the life experiences that you have had. Take a moment or two to rank the elements of identity based on your personal feelings and preferences. We will call this your primary element(s) of identity.

THE STEP BY STEP

 Consider the list of the elements of identity shown in Figure 2–5.

 Review the meanings for each and rank each in order from 1 to 5, with 1 being the element of identity with which you have the most connection and 5 being the least. Utilize what you have written for each of the elements in your personal spaces earlier in this chapter.

_____	Cognitive Identity: Your personal perspective of the achievements, improvements, and activity of your mind.
_____	Cultural Identity: Your personal perspective of society, culture, and personal relationships.
_____	Emotional Identity: Your personal perspective of how your feelings guide who you are and how you see the world.
_____	Physical Identity: Your personal perspective of how you value your body.
_____	Spiritual Identity: Your personal perspective of your religious, ethical, and/or sacred beliefs.

FIGURE 2–5
Ranking the Elements of Identity

Reflections

Having ranked the elements of identity based on your comfort and personal preference, consider the following questions:

Some of the elements probably seem pretty clear to you. If there are areas that are unclear, why are they unclear?

What can you reflect on in your life experience that has prevented you from fully developing these elements?

Personal Space

_____

_____

_____

_____

_____

_____

_____

_____

_____

_____

_____

_____

_____

_____

_____

_____

MAKING GOOD DECISIONS

Now that you have a deeper understanding of the elements of identity and how you personally connect with each, let's apply some of this newly discovered knowledge to a real-life scenario.

AIMEE'S DILEMMA

Aimee is an entry-level manager at a small company. Her workplace is close to her home, and this gives her ample opportunity to spend lots of time with family and friends. Her lifestyle is comfortable and allows her great flexibility. Aimee is very active in the community, including activities with the local recreation center and Habitat for Humanity, a community service group. She places great stock in her ability to make time for family and considers family members her number one priority.

While her managerial position is ideal from the perspective of her personal and family life, professionally Aimee is bored. She does not particularly enjoy going to work, because it is not an intellectually stimulating experience. Oftentimes she feels that the work environment does not challenge or satisfy her.

As fate would have it, Aimee is offered an opportunity to move to a position at a competing, larger company that will challenge her intellectually and

> " ————————
> The self is not something
> ready-made, but something in
> continuous formation through
> choice of action."
>
> —*JOHN DEWEY*

professionally. This new position will bring better income and carries with it a sizable increase in responsibility. Unfortunately, the position requires a lengthy commute, would pull her away from her highly valued family time, and would lessen the overall flexibility in her life.

Aimee is facing a decision that will impact her family, her career, and her overall existence. For her, this truly is a life-altering moment.

What should Aimee do? What things should she consider in making her decision? What types of issues would be important for you to consider if this was a choice that you had to make? What areas of your identity would be most impacted by having to make this decision? What aspects of her personal journey are important for Aimee to consider in making this choice?

An important factor in effectively utilizing your personal vision is having a decision-making process that will guide you through situations like the one Aimee is facing, one that will challenge you to consider what elements in your life guide you the most when you need to make important choices.

MAKING SELF-INFORMED DECISIONS

All of your life, you have been told that when you need to make a decision, it should be an "informed" one. Oftentimes the definition of *informed* is driven by external factors and other people. For example, in Aimee's situation, she probably would be advised to research the new company that she is considering. She would be told to get all of the details regarding salary and benefits, work environment, supervisory structure, and other professional considerations. Friends and family would probably encourage her to consider whether the job is a good "fit" for her and to trust her gut instinct. The idea of personal fit and going with her gut creates questions about whether the values and ethics of the company fit her way of being or personal style. A self-informed decision requires a thorough understanding of personal values and motivators in all aspects of your life. You need to know how your personal identity areas shape who you are and how they impact your personal life journey.

A SELF-INFORMED DECISION REQUIRES A THOROUGH UNDERSTANDING OF

PERSONAL VALUES AND MOTIVATORS IN ALL ASPECTS OF YOUR LIFE.

To make decisions that will enhance your life and be congruent with your values, you need to have a deep understanding of what motivates your core being. To be self-informed, you must understand how a given challenge impacts your whole self—your mind, body, spirit, heart, and relationships. Self-informed solutions are then balanced and consistent with your personal vision.

The decisions that you make on a daily basis sometimes impact the moment, and at times can impact the rest of your life. The tough part is that you really do not know how a decision made today will impact you tomorrow. Throughout your development as a person, you have set up personal systems to weigh the importance of every decision that you make, but in the end you may wrongly estimate how much or little a choice will affect you.

Regardless of the decision before you, there are questions that you can ask yourself that will help you to make a good choice. Everyone has internal mechanisms that weigh the pros and cons of every choice. These internal mechanisms force you to explore your inner motivations and ultimately guide you in making a choice with which you are comfortable.

activity 3 HOW DO YOU MAKE DECISIONS?

ACTIVITY PURPOSE

This activity will help you to determine the questions that you ask yourself when you are required to make an important decision. ◼

Sometimes the questions we pose to ourselves in answering life's questions are self-motivated, and at other times the way we make our decisions lies directly in how others will be impacted. What are the questions that you ask yourself when you are at a crossroads in your personal journey?

THE STEP BY STEP

In the space provided, write down some of the questions that you ask yourself when it comes time to make decisions. Start by writing a brief description of an unresolved situation that is affecting your life now. If one does not come to mind, look back to Aimee's story and create a list of questions that you would pose to yourself if you were in her shoes. Then think of a situation that relates to you and repeat the process.

Write a brief description of the situation/problem/question that you wish to resolve. Pick a situation when you were required to make a decision that felt very important to you; it could be a current situation or one from your past.

_____

_____

_____

_____

_____

_____

_____

_____

_____

_____

_____

_____

_____

_____

Write the first question that you would ask yourself here (do not answer the question yet):

_____

_____

_____

_____

_____

_____

Why is this question so important to you? Why is it important that you have an answer to this question?

_____

_____

_____

_____

_____

_____

Write the second question that you would ask yourself here:

_____

_____

_____

_____

_____

Why is this question so important to you? Why is it important that you have an answer to this question?

_____

_____

_____

_____

_____

_____

Write the third question that you would ask yourself here:

_____

_____

_____

_____

_____

Why is this question so important to you? Why is it important that you have an answer to this question?

_____

_____

_____

_____

_____

Write the fourth question that you would ask yourself here:

_____

_____

_____

_____

Why is this question so important to you? Why is it important that you have an answer to this question?

_____

_____

_____

_____

_____

_____

Write the fifth question that you would ask yourself here:

_____

_____

_____

_____

_____

_____

Why is this question so important to you? Why is it important that you have an answer to this question?

_____

_____

_____

_____

_____

_____

Reflections

Identifying your most important questions and considering why they are so important provides definition and direction to your problem-solving process.

Now that you have created five questions that will guide your decision making process in this situation, do you notice any themes in the types of questions that you ask?

Are your questions internally focused or focused on your environment?

Do you tend to think more of your personal life or your occupational life?

Do spiritual considerations come into play?

You will answer your own questions in the next activity.

Personal Space

_____

_____

_____

_____

_____

_____

_____

_____

_____

_____

_____

_____

_____

_____

_____

_____

_____

_____

activity 4   THE FIVE WHYS

The next activity will assist you in clarifying the root of where questions that you ask yourself come from. You will find that they come from your deepest values. If you consider that the roots of a tree feed the trunk, branches, and leaves, so too do your values feed the questions that you ask and the curiosities that you hold.

THE STEP BY STEP

In the following space, write the first question that you decided on from the last activity:

_____

_____

_____

_____

_____

_____

Now answer the question in the following space:

_____

_____

_____

_____

_____

_____

_____

ACTIVITY PURPOSE

This activity will help you to understand the clarifying qualities of the "five whys" technique. ◼

Now consider the answer that you just created and ask yourself "why?" Write the answer in the following space:

_____

_____

_____

_____

_____

_____

Now consider the answer to the first "why" and ask "why?" again. Write your answer here:

_____

_____

_____

_____

_____

_____

Now consider the answer to the third "why" and ask "why?" again. Write your answer here:

_____

_____

_____

_____

_____

_____

Repeat a fourth time:

_____

_____

_____

_____

_____

_____

And finally, a fifth "why?"

_____

_____

_____

_____

_____

_____

Example

If you think back to Aimee's situation, you can gain insight as to how the five whys can be helpful.

Situation: Whether or not to take the new employment opportunity.

Question 1: How will this decision impact my connection with my family, which is very important to me?
Answer: It will prevent me from seeing my children as much as I have been able to.

Why 1: Why will it prevent me from seeing my children as much as I have been able to?
Answer: I will have to commute and work longer hours in order to adjust to the new position.

Why 2: Why will I have to work longer hours in order to adjust to the new position?
Answer: I will have to work longer hours in order to adjust because I am nervous about this change.

Why 3: Why am I nervous about this change?
Answer: I am nervous about this change because I have been in my current job for so long.

Why 4: Why have I been in my current job for so long?
Answer: I have been in my current job for so long because I dislike taking risks, and I dislike change.

Why 5: Why do I dislike taking risks and changing?
Answer: I dislike taking risks and changing because it is a change to my routine.

Solution: Aimee needs to recognize her dislike for change and weigh that against her feelings of losing contact with her family.

Reflections

Asking "why?" at least five times when making a decision brings you closer and closer to the root of the situation. Usually this will take five whys . . . sometimes more . . . and sometimes less. The answer to your fifth why has most likely brought you to a core value of some sort. This represents a driving and important quality about yourself that you need to verify before answering your initial

> " I can't understand why people are frightened of new ideas. I'm frightened of the old ones."
>
> —*JOHN CAGE (1912–1992)*

question. Feel free to answer the other questions that you created in the preceding activity with the five whys as well.

Professionals from all walks of life use this technique when attempting to identify the "root cause" of situations that they face. You can use this same management technique in your own life. Understanding the roots of your questions will help you understand how you balance the multiple elements of your identity.

How did answering the multiple levels of "why" questions help you to gain clarity with your questions?

How did your root question change as you continued asking "why?"

What do you realize about your initial questions that has changed?

Personal Space

_____

_____

_____

_____

_____

_____

_____

_____

_____

_____

_____

_____

_____

_____

_____

_____

_____

THE VISION PYRAMID

The Personal Vision Creation Model explores each of your elements of identity as described earlier. The six triangles pointing inwardly represent the Vision Pyramid applied to each of the identity elements and the journey that you take in developing your identity. The center of the model is where the five pyramids point. This is _your_ center; it is the source of _your_ personal vision.

Figure 2–6 shows the Vision Pyramid as it applies to each of the elements of your personal identity (cognitive, cultural, emotional, physical, and spiritual).

FIGURE 2–6
The Vision Pyramid

This journey points you in the direction of self-discovery. Each level of the pyramid has a specific focus and asks different things of you as you develop each area of identity.

IDENTITY—LEVEL 1 OF THE VISION PYRAMID

The visioning process begins by exploring each identity element. This level is where you will spend the majority of your time, and it is the largest layer of the pyramid. There will be numerous experiences and activities during which you will discover yourself and your values. The hardest work and the most rewards come at level 1 of the Vision Pyramid.

THE HARDEST WORK AND THE MOST REWARDS COME AT LEVEL 1

OF THE VISION PYRAMID.

VALUES—LEVEL 2 OF THE VISION PYRAMID

Once you have a clear sense of your identity in any given element, you move to creating core values. Core values answer the question "Why am I the way I am and what should I do about it?" This is where you apply your own judgments to how you should live your life. For example, after exploring the physical identity element, you might establish that you feel healthy and alive. What are you? You are healthy and alive! A value that you may create based on this identity characteristic is to live life to its fullest.

GOALS—LEVEL 3 OF THE VISION PYRAMID

Core values set the framework for developing personal goals and mission statements. Personal goals answer the question "How do you live by your values?" The more specific, measurable, realistic, and timely you make your goals, the better the opportunity you will have to create positive change in your life. In this step you will determine how to live out your values. Where does this take your life?

MISSION—LEVEL 4 OF THE VISION PYRAMID

Mission statements provide a synopsis of the direction in which your life is headed. You may think of mission statements like a map of your life strategy. Missions are short, written descriptions of where you want to go in life. They establish what is most important to you and prioritize goals. By establishing a mission in each of your elements of identity, you pave the way for creating a personal vision!

BY ESTABLISHING A MISSION IN EACH OF YOUR ELEMENTS OF IDENTITY,

YOU PAVE THE WAY FOR CREATING A PERSONAL VISION!

> " The real voyage of discovery consists not in seeking new landscapes but in having new eyes."
>
> —*MARCEL PROUST*

VISION

The elements of identity point inwardly toward your center; they are the source of your personal vision. Visions capture the meaning behind all of the elements of your identity and the journey that you take to discover them. There is no specified format for a personal vision. You set the rules. This is the most deeply personal part of the book. You are free to represent yourself any way that you see fit.

JOURNEY VS. DESTINATION

To actively engage with this book, you will need to tap into your creative reserves and be ready to take on a new perspective of yourself. This is about the journey, not the destination. Your journey will include self-exploration, discovery of new values with which to live your life, and visions of hopes and dreams that you may have never thought possible. You control the progress through the workbook, and only you will know when you have reached an end. Imagine, a book in which you get to write your own personal story!

In telling your own story, do not short-change yourself; you are the author! While you will want to focus on getting to the creation of personal vision, take the time to fully experience the journey. Remember the old adage about stopping to smell the roses on your journey through life? The more you focus on the journey (and smell the roses that you missed), the more this visioning process will impact all parts of your life. If you are completing the workbook within a development team or as a class assignment, your facilitator or instructor may create boundaries and time-lines for the activities. Be aware that you may need to come back to parts of the book after the "assignment" is done.

The journey toward discovering your personal vision is more important than the actual vision you end up with. Initially, this may seem a bit odd. It is human nature to want to finish and be proud of what you accomplished. No doubt, when you complete the relevant activities in this book and discover your

> " A process cannot be understood by stopping it. Understanding must move with the flow of the process, must join it and flow with it."
>
> —*FRANK HERBERT*

The Step by Step	Each activity will explain the tasks that you will need to do to complete the activity. It is important that you follow the instructions as provided in the book. Each activity is designed to maximize your experience.
Reflections	This section is designed to help you take a step back and reflect on the bigger picture of what you are working toward in each activity. Questions are posed to help you relate the activity to your personal identity. This is your opportunity to think about the purpose and wisdom gained by each activity.
Personal Space	You will always be provided space to journal your thoughts at the end of each activity. Jot down self-observations, answer questions, and make notes for yourself. Think of this space as your travel journal. Use the space as you wish. Remember it is the journey—not the destination—that you seek.

FIGURE 2–7
Personal Vision Activity Primer

vision, you will feel a great sense of accomplishment. This is quite natural. However, it is the journey of self-exploration that will add the greatest value to your life. For example, imagine going on a long vacation. What is more valuable, the journey to new destinations or the pile of scenic pictures you have when you return? Anyone can pick up a travel book to see scenic pictures. The impact lies in the experience of actually exploring new destinations. The pictures are mere representations of the things that you saw, touched, tasted, smelled, and so forth.

HOW THIS BOOK WORKS

This book is packed with fun and introspective activities. Each activity follows a specific format intended to give you clear directions, ample space to write down reactions, and process questions to consider on completion of each activity. To create clarity, read the description given in Figure 2–7 about how the activities in this book are organized.

Although the activities presented should create a strong foundation for your personal visioning experience, you may find that you want to change the activity to better suit you. If you are able to reconstruct an activity that we have created in a way that encourages more growth on your part, then please do so!

VISION PYRAMID ACTIVITY PRIMER

At the end of each identity chapter there is a step-by-step guide through the visioning process. You begin by finding 10 phrases, themes, and/or ideas that regularly appear throughout the notes from activities that you chose to do. The personal spaces at the end of each activity are great locations to look for these

10 phrases, themes, and/or ideas. Next, you will consolidate your list to establish your core values.

AT THE END OF EACH IDENTITY CHAPTER THERE IS A STEP-BY-STEP GUIDE

THROUGH THE VISIONING PROCESS.

Ask "why?" repeatedly to each of the phrases, themes, and/or ideas that you select until you isolate their core meaning. You will notice gaps between who you are now and who you want to be. Create personal goals that are specific, measurable, realistic, and timely to close these gaps. Think of your personal goals as temporary action plans to get you going in the right direction. The direction you are headed is summarized in mission statements. Mission statements are as unique as the individual creating them. There is no right or wrong grammatical format that you should follow. Missions can be as detailed or as broad as you would like them to be. The format is less important than the statement it makes regarding the direction of your life.

Upon completing activities for all of the elements of identity, you will be left with the task of creating your five overall core values and personal vision. If you have invested in the process (the journey), the vision will become clear very quickly. You will find that you have created a detailed description of who you are, what motivates you, and what values lead you in life.

Before you begin exploring the five elements of identity, you need to better assess and understand what personal values are and how they impact your life. Chapter 3 will further explain the concept of core values and will give you an opportunity to select values that are important to you now.

Developing Your Personal Values

HAPPINESS IS THAT STATE OF CONSCIOUSNESS WHICH PROCEEDS

FROM THE ACHIEVEMENT OF ONE'S VALUES.

■

—AYN RAND

WHAT ARE PERSONAL VALUES?

A personal value is a principle, standard, or quality that you consider worthwhile or desirable. This chapter is designed to introduce you to the concept of personal values and prime your energies to focus on discovering your own personal values.

A PERSONAL VALUE IS A PRINCIPLE, STANDARD, OR QUALITY THAT

YOU CONSIDER WORTHWHILE OR DESIRABLE.

Personal values form the criterion for evaluating what is important in your journey through life. Values range from basic ideas, such as a belief in honesty, simplicity, and integrity, to more psychological values, such as concern for others, trust in others, and harmony of purpose. You may have values about family relationships (example: how children should behave toward adults), about work relationships (example: how quickly one should respond to an e-mail or voice mail), and about other personal and relationship issues (example: how we should treat other animals and life forms). Your personal values dictate who you are, the kinds of decisions you make, and how you react in times of crisis. The patterns of your responses form your personality, how others perceive you, and how you perceive yourself.

Values play an important role in your life. First, values provide the framework for choosing your actions. You make commitments to yourself to behave in a particular way based on your values; for instance, "I will tell the truth if they ask." The criterion for choosing almost every action you make is based on values. Essentially, values act as shortcuts in your mind. Rather than contemplating all of the possible responses to every given situation, values establish preset responses to similar situations. For example, when asked for the truth, if you value honesty, it is simple to decide to tell the truth. You don't have to spend a lot of time contemplating options. The more you know about your internal shortcuts or values, the better prepared you are to understand how they motivate and lead you.

Second, acting on your values consistently makes it easier for others to understand you. People are constantly looking for patterns in your behavior to better predict what you will do in the future. For example, when you consistently tell the truth, others are likely to assume that you are trustworthy. Living your values helps others relate to you better. Likewise, congruent actions regarding your personal values establish your own sense of self-worth. The values that you will define in this book will become the foundation for your personal vision.

Finally, your personal values form the criteria with which you evaluate others' behaviors. How should other people act? This is a very different question than how you should act. Personal values help you judge what is right, just, and good in the world and are important to the creation of a sense of social justice, personal ethics, and standards. Values help you to understand other people, avoid danger or discomfort, and function in group settings.

PERSONAL VALUES HELP YOU JUDGE WHAT IS RIGHT, JUST, AND GOOD

IN THE WORLD.

ORGANIZATIONAL AND PERSONAL VALUES

Just as individuals subscribe to personal values, so do institutions. Here are some examples of how different organizations use values to guide their operations:

- One of Toyota's core values is quality. This value drives Toyota to produce vehicles that hold up longer with fewer defects than many of its competitors.

- Apple Computer values simplicity and innovative design; its computers and other products are user friendly and instantly recognizable. Apple's innovative design has propelled it from a company in disrepair to a leader in small consumer electronics.

- Syracuse University utilizes five core values (quality, caring, diversity, innovation, and service) in the way it implements its educational mission, administrative functions, and academic teachings.

In all three of these organizations, values are the foundation for their competitive advantage. Oftentimes, success in the marketplace is based on how unified an organization can be when rallying around a few central values. Values drive success.

Values also drive success in your own life. Committing to act on the values you already believe, or searching to adopt new values that fit your life, is an incredibly powerful process. Organizations are pulled in many directions, and life pulls you in multiple and competing directions as well. Values act as the glue that holds you together. Without values, you are likely to follow the direction of other people, who may prioritize what's important in very different ways than you might.

You can find unity in your own life through the practice of following your values in all situations. Decisions become easier when you continually apply your values. The best way to understand what is most important to you is to determine your priorities. Likewise, others understand you better because the patterns of your behaviors are consistent.

If you are working through *the Personal Vision Workbook* in order to create team core values or a team vision, you will find that the synchronization of all of your teammates' values will create strong direction for your organization. If you are completing this workbook with a significant other, you will create opportunities to recognize how your core values and beliefs mesh.

activity   THE PERSONAL VALUES SORTER

The following activity is designed to introduce you to personal values. Allow your mind to be free to explore the ideas and phrases listed. You may find that the beliefs and motivators that you hold most sacred are not as apparent as you would have thought. Although the activities in this workbook are optional to some degree, this is one that we strongly encourage you to complete, because it will create a foundation for many of the others.

ACTIVITY PURPOSE

This activity will give you a basic understanding of which values are most important to you. ■

THE STEP BY STEP

1. In figure 3–1, you will find a list of values. You can also find a larger print version of this table on the Delmar Online Companion website. Remove the page and cut out each of the values individually, including the blanks, or print and cut out the web version.

2. On a flat surface, spread out the values so that you can see them all.

3. Read over the values carefully and think about how each pertains to your life.

4. If there are missing values that are important to you, write them in the blank pieces that you also cut out.

5. Select the 10 values that are the least important to you. That is, which 10 values, if discarded, would have the least impact on your life? Place these 10 in a discard pile.

6. From the remaining values, select the 15 that are most important to you. Write these 15 values in the appropriate spaces in the worksheet following the values list (Figure 3–2).

7. Which values are critical to your existence? Which values can you live without? Narrow the 15 values that you have selected to the five most important values.

COMMON PERSONAL VALUES

accomplishment	diversity	inclusiveness	pleasure	simplicity
accountability	duty	influence	popularity	sincerity
accuracy	education	inner peace	positive attitude	skill
achievement	efficiency	innovation	power	solidarity
adventure	empowerment	improvement	practicality	speed
aspiration	equality	integrity	preservation	spirit-in-life
attitude	excellence	intuition	prestige	stability
authenticity	expression	involvement	pride	standardization
authority	fairness	joy & delight	privacy	status
autonomy	faith	justice	prosperity/wealth	strength
beauty	fame	knowledge	punctuality	style
challenge	family	leadership	purity	success
change	fate	learning	quality	support
chastity/purity	fitness	leisure	rationality	systemization
cleanliness	flair	love-romance	recognition	teamwork
collaboration	force	love-care	regularity	timeliness
commitment	freedom	love-concern	rehabilitation	tolerance
communication	free will	loyalty	reliability	tradition
community	fun	meaning	resourcefulness	tranquility
competence	generosity	merit	respect	trust
competition	giving/charity	mobility	responsibility	truth
concern for others	global view	money	responsiveness	utility
conformity	goodness	nonviolence	results-oriented	variety
courage	gratitude	nurturing	risk-taking	well-being
conviction	hard work	openness	rootedness	wellness
cooperation	harmony	optimism	rule of law	wisdom
creativity	health	patriotism	safety	
customer satisfaction	helpfulness	peace	satisfying others	
decisiveness	heroism	perfection	security	
democracy	heritage	performance	selflessness	
determination	honesty	persistence	self-reliance	
discipline	honor	personal growth	seriousness	
discover	hope	philosophy	service	
discovery	humor	pioneer spirit	sexuality	

FIGURE 3–1 Common Personal Values

8   Write these five values in the appropriate space on the worksheet. Keep these values in mind as you complete the rest of this book. Place all of the values into an envelope, and keep the envelope with the book. You will need this envelope later!

VALUES WORKSHEET

What are the top 15 values that you selected from the list?

Write them in the following spaces:

_____   _____   _____

_____   _____   _____

_____   _____   _____

_____   _____   _____

_____   _____   _____

What are your top five values?

Prioritize, merge, or consolidate the 15 values above to the five personal values that are the most important to you:

_____   _____   _____

_____   _____

Define your top five personal values:

Now that you have settled on five values that are very important to you, it is time to define them a bit. After writing the five values in the following spaces, write a brief description of why these values are so important to you.

Value: _____
     Define:

Value: _____
     Define:

Value: _____
     Define:

Value: _____
     Define:

Value: _____
     Define:

FIGURE 3–2
Personal Values Worksheet

Suggestions

- Some values may seem repetitive or closely related to each other. Choose one and discard the other(s) that shares the same meaning for you. This may be an easy way to narrow the list.

- Don't get stuck on a value's textbook definition. What does the word mean to you? Your own definition is the most important.

- Keep this activity personal. Seeking advice from others will only skew your results. You are on your own for this activity!

- When deciding what values are most important to you, consider which values would guide you best in a majority of situations. Which of these would you be least willing to give up?

- Review your results two days later. Check to see if your top five values are still vital to you.

Reflections

This activity is designed to get you to think in the language of values. As you proceed with the many activities in the book, you can utilize this list and your prioritization. The key will be to notice which values surface frequently, which will help you to zero in on your personal core values.

If you reviewed your top five personal values after two days, did they change?

What themes do you see in your top five personal values?

What themes do you see in the values you discarded?

How do you make decisions by the top five personal values?

What decisions have you made that were in conflict with these values?

Personal Space

_____

_____

_____

_____

_____

_____

_____

_____

_____

_____

_____

_____

_____

_____

_____

_____

YOUR NEXT STEP!

The remainder of this workbook will help you to define your identity areas and bring into sharp focus why your decisions should demonstrate your values.

By completing the value-sorting activity in this chapter, you will be more effective with the forthcoming activities. The list of values that you created will be important throughout your visioning experience. You can reopen the envelope, dump the contents out, and use the contents to better understand what you are learning about yourself at every step of the voyage!

You've completed the first three chapters; you now have the critical navigational tools to begin the exploration of your personal vision. You know what the elements of your identity are and how the journey is vital to your development. You also have a foundational definition of personal values and some experience defining your values. Now it is time to delve deeply into each element to get a clear picture of where you wish to take your life.

Although cognitive identity is covered in the next chapter, it may not be your next step. In Chapter 2, you learned a bit about each identity area and you ranked these areas according to personal preference. Start with your most comfortable and/or relevant identity area. This will give you an opportunity to begin the development of your identity areas on recognizable ground. Remember, this is your journey—you do not have to proceed in our order!

If you are completing _the Personal Vision Workbook_ with a work team or as a classroom experience, your facilitator or instructor may direct you to a certain element first. This is certainly okay! Given the potential for group development, it may be more effective for the entire group or class to work on a particular element of identity together. If you are completing the workbook with a significant other, you should choose together where to begin.

Have fun!

The Cognitive Identity Area

THE TRUE SIGN OF INTELLIGENCE IS NOT KNOWLEDGE BUT IMAGINATION.

■

—ALBERT EINSTEIN

COGNITIVE IDENTITY

Cognitive identity encompasses how your mind processes information, which areas of the world most interest you, and the occupational path that you will travel. It is your cognitive identity that motivates discovery as a means to fulfill your curiosities. Think of the books that you like to read, interest areas that you wish to research, or new skills that you have been wanting to develop. This desire to better understand your world is important, because it will help to define your intellectual interests and potential career path. These interests also define your cognitive identity.

Using the list provided in Figure 4–1 on the next page, take a moment to define those things that you most like to investigate. What are your greatest intellectual interests (for example, physics, business management, nature, music, art)?

The five things that first came to mind are topics that help to define your cognitive identity. If you hear of these things in conversation, or on a television program, or even in casual conversation, your ears perk up.

Developing your cognitive identity will cause you to bring facts, figures, and concepts that you read or learn into conversations. New knowledge in an area that interests you is exciting! This is the part of you that looks for something that will stimulate your mind, move your career, and/or quench your curiosities.

Your cognitive identity includes your intellect and your career/occupational path. The way you think, the way you process information, and what makes your mind tick all motivate you in your eventual choice of

Your personal perspective of the achievements, improvements, and exercise of your mind.

The symbol used to signify cognitive identity comes from an ancient apothecary symbol for hermaphrodite (neither male nor female) and gives special prominence to the development of the mind, or intellect (indicated by the double curve above the central circle). The crossed lines at the bottom of the circle indicate a growth process.

```
┌─────────────────────────────────────────────────────┐
│  My Intellectual Interests                            │
│                                                       │
│        1. _____    │
│                                                       │
│        2. _____    │
│                                                       │
│        3. _____    │
│                                                       │
│        4. _____    │
│                                                       │
│        5. _____    │
│                                                       │
└─────────────────────────────────────────────────────┘
```

FIGURE 4–1
My Intellectual Interests

occupation. If you have a job or occupation that conflicts with your interests or does not connect to the way your mind works, you may be unsatisfied. Unfortunately, many people hold jobs or are in higher education studying subjects that do not match their interests or intellect—and that creates a big challenge. Although you can force yourself to learn uninteresting information, it certainly takes more effort than learning about areas of natural interest.

At some point in your life, you may work at a job or study a subject that holds little interest. Many times this lack of interest forces you to process information in ways that are incongruent with your cognitive identity. Similar to your body, you can train your mind to think or process information differently. However, it takes significantly more time and energy. Finding a profession, occupation, or field of study that is congruent with your cognitive identity will create positive results. Knowing your cognitive identity will help you choose a profession or occupation that is most fulfilling.

> I happen to feel that the degree of a person's intelligence is directly reflected by the number of conflicting attitudes she can bring to bear on the same topic."
>
> —LISA ALTHER

KNOWLEDGE, INTELLECT, AND WISDOM

There are three critical components to your cognitive identity: knowledge, intellect, and wisdom. These three components make up what you know, how you learn it, and when you apply your knowledge in the world. Apply the following analogy to understand cognitive identity. Imagine your mind as a large storage center. Each cell within this storage center is designed to store certain things: names, numbers, facts, concepts, images, memories, and so forth. The information stored in your mind is knowledge. Knowledge is limitless. Everybody's storage center (mind) is designed differently. Some are able to store more names than numbers. Others store more concepts and images. Each storage unit is unique.

How information is put in or stored in your mind is intellect. Think of your intellect as the shipping and receiving department of your storage center. Intellect determines what information comes in, where it is stored, and how it is accessed. Intelligence then is how quickly, accurately, and with what level of complexity orders can be fulfilled in your mind.

Finally, wisdom refers to when the knowledge is applied. Applying the analogy, wisdom refers to the use of the things that are stored in your storage center. It follows then that one can acquire a great deal of knowledge but be no better off without the practical application of this knowledge. Think of this as book-smart but street-dumb. Wise people know when to use their knowledge. As we all know, however, knowledgeable people are not always particularly wise!

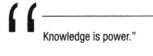

> " Knowledge is power."
>
> —*FRANCIS BACON*

THE POWER OF KNOWLEDGE

You've probably heard the adage "knowledge is power." In keeping with this idea, the way to gain more power and influence in your life is to maximize the storage of knowledge in your mind. What fits in your mind best and hence reflects your cognitive identity? Look at your cognitive identity as being like a blueprint of the knowledge storage units within your mind. You can maximize your knowledge by simply recognizing how information best fits in your mind.

You may feel that the cognitive identity element really seems suited for people who have completed their occupational training (apprenticeship, college, training institute, etc.) and are "on the job." But there are many other ways in which this identity element connects to you regardless of your current occupational status. Your cognitive identity began to develop the moment you stacked your first block, if not earlier. From the very beginning, your uniqueness helped to determine where your intellect would take you.

KNOWLEDGE

is the intellectual accumulation of information that you have acquired through education, training, and experience.

KNOWLEDGE OFTEN SERVES AS A SOCIAL MARKER, AND PROFESSIONALLY

YOU SELF-SELECT BY ACKNOWLEDGING WHETHER OR NOT YOU HAVE

THE SKILLS TO FUNCTION IN A GIVEN OCCUPATION.

Knowledge often serves as a social marker, and professionally you self-select by acknowledging whether or not you have the skills to function in a given occupation. There are many different ways to be intelligent, and as you will learn later, none are more important than any others. Some people do fit certain occupational choices better. It is a matter of understanding your areas of strength and using them to bring success.

As you focus on your cognitive identity, you will discover whether your current career or future career plans match your cognitive core values. You will be able to better utilize your intellectual time and energy. In essence, you will synchronize your own mind.

WISDOM

Wisdom refers to your ability to make sound decisions based on experiences from your past. It is wisdom that allows you to develop common sense, and it serves as the part of your cognitive identity that you feel the most pleasure in sharing.

WISDOM

is your ability to make sound decisions based on experiences from your past.

Wisdom levels the cognitive playing field. Knowledge and intellect can seem a bit presumptuous and assume a certain level of education, training, or formal instruction. Wisdom, on the other hand, is about the good use of your mental abilities. It is about applying the lessons you have learned to your everyday life. Wisdom is so unique to each individual that it is difficult to measure, and nearly impossible to compare—yet we all know a wise person when we meet one.

WISDOM IS SO UNIQUE TO EACH INDIVIDUAL THAT IT IS DIFFICULT

TO MEASURE, AND NEARLY IMPOSSIBLE TO COMPARE—YET WE ALL

KNOW A WISE PERSON WHEN WE MEET ONE.

WISDOM AND BURNING BOOKS

Once there was a well-known philosopher and scholar who devoted herself to the study of Zen for many years. On the day she finally attained enlightenment, she took all of her books out into the yard and burned them all.

It would seem that the Zen master defies wisdom with the burning of books that taught her so much. The lesson learned, however, is that without good use of knowledge, it fails to become part of a person's wisdom; it would simply remain pages in a book. Upon enlightenment, the Zen scholar was able to bring the studied concepts into consciousness and use. In turn, she was the wiser for it.

As with the Zen master, once you have gained wisdom, it is with you for the rest of your life. Once you gain that wisdom, you will never have to study it again.

Parents, grandparents, and mentors do not have a monopoly on wisdom. True, it is often our elders whom we look to and respect for their wisdom. However, if you search your thoughts and feelings, you may find others (such as your peers) who you feel hold a wise perspective from which you find yourself learning. It would stand to reason then that there are people in your life who look up to you. Think of areas in your life where people respect you, where you are asked about your knowledge, and where you are asked for advice. For example, maybe you are asked for your opinion about certain topics or for help with personal problems and relationships. If your peers are seeking you out for advice in important areas, they probably see you as a wise person.

> "Science is organized knowledge. Wisdom is organized life."
>
> —IMMANUEL KANT

DEVELOPING COGNITIVE IDENTITY

The accumulation and the understanding of knowledge, intellect, and wisdom are the cornerstones of developing your cognitive identity. There is a need to understand the lessons that you have learned in your past, an ability to place current cognitive challenges into useful perspective, and the foresight to know where your pursuits of thought will take you.

COGNITIVE IDENTITY FOCAL POINTS AND ACTIVITIES

Your cognitive identity is rooted in how you use your mind to enhance your intellect, knowledge, and career path.

As you complete the activities in this chapter, which are summarized in the following list, remember to keep track of reoccurring themes which present themselves to you. What types of values are you seeing repeatedly? How do your discoveries in these activities help you to understand yourself better? What topics reappear as areas that are intriguing? What are you learning about how you learn and how you best take in and store information?

Activity 1: The Wisdom Wheel. As we have discussed, wisdom refers to your ability to effectively use your acquired knowledge from past experiences in your everyday life. This activity will help you to connect important experiences in your life with the lessons (wisdom) that you have learned as a result.

Activity 2: Your Multiple Intelligences. Howard Gardner proposed a theory that people have multiple types of intelligence. In this activity, you will rank Gardner's multiple intelligences for yourself and will learn about how they shape who you are.

Activity 3: Job Interviews for Your Life. Most likely, you have been involved in at least one job interview. This activity turns the table on the traditional interview and asks you to interview those people closest to you about what they think a good career for you would be. Questions are provided to start, and you can add others to fit you more specifically.

Activity 4: Career Kaleidoscope. What is the right career path for you? This activity will bring skills that you possess and activities that you like to engage in into sharp focus. You will discover that knowing what you like to do will lead you to a career that will bring you satisfaction and success.

ACTIVITY PURPOSE

To better understand how your pearls of wisdom help to shape your identity. ■

" The mistakes of the fool are known to the world, but not to himself. The mistakes of the wise man are known to himself, but not to the world."

—CHARLES COLTON

activity 1 **THE WISDOM WHEEL**

Your cumulative wisdom is a result of the experiences in your life that you deem important enough to consider as "learned lessons." These moments in your life have great impact and have affected your decision making ever since. These experiences may come at a crucial decision-making point in your life or may simply be an "a-ha" moment that you had while reading a motivating passage, listening to a piece of music, or viewing an image. In sharing your sense of wisdom, you demonstrate what is most important to you.

In this activity, you will consider past experiences and determine the pearls of wisdom that you carry around with you. You will also better understand the origins of these pearls and identify the personal motivators that come from them.

THE STEP BY STEP

1. Begin this activity by finding a quiet place where you can focus on your personal history. You may have already engaged in some activities in this workbook that have asked you to think about your significant past experiences; referring to those notes will be very useful.

2. Write four detailed, personal situations/stories (Figure 4–2) during which you learned an important life lesson, realized a fact of life that altered your beliefs, or had an awakening of some sort.

3. Now summarize your stories into shortened symbolic stories. Place these four symbolic stories on the outer ring of the wisdom wheel (Figure 4–3).

4. Now put into words the wisdom that you gained as a result of your experiences. Make each pearl of wisdom short and to the point, but phrase it in a way that helps you to retain the story that comes with the lesson.

Example

Here's an example of a personal story:

Personal Story

I remember when I was seven my grandfather and I were walking in the forest near his home, a place where we frequently walked together. Walking with my grandfather was important to me, because it was through these walks that I learned a great deal about the trees and animals. We came upon a small deer that had been wounded by a coyote and was barely hanging on. I remember being horrified by the sight and asked my grandfather why God would allow this to happen.

My grandfather explained that all creatures must die, even if it sometimes seems unfair. He told me that the deer had

---

Personal Story 1:

Personal Story 2:

Personal Story 3:

Personal Story 4:

FIGURE 4–2
Your Stories of Wisdom

lived the life it was supposed to have lived and it was its time to move on.

Symbolic Story

My grandfather taught me one day in the woods that even an innocent creature such as a deer has a natural life as well as death.

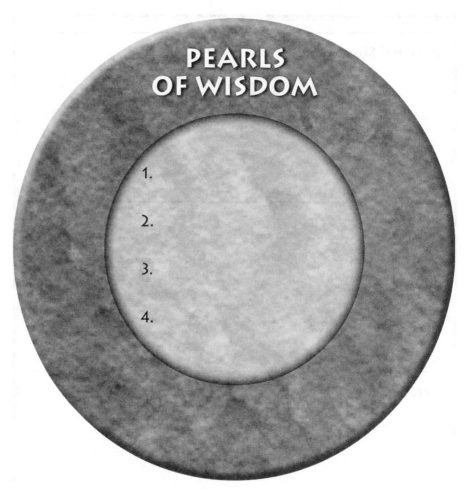

FIGURE 4–3 The Wisdom Wheel

Pearl of Wisdom

> There is a natural order to life; all things happen for a reason.

Try to write your personal stories in detail, because doing so will help you to find deeper meaning to the wisdom you gained. Try to bring the emotions that you felt during your experiences into your stories.

Write out your four personal stories in Figure 4–2.

Next, in the wisdom wheel shown in Figure 4–3, create four symbolic stories for your personal stories in the outer ring, and then write your pearls of wisdom in the center of the circle.

Reflections

Now that you have your pearls of wisdom, consider how they tie into your cognitive identity. As we said earlier, wisdom is your ability to utilize intellect to make sound decisions based on useful experiences from your past.

How does each pearl of wisdom impact the way that you interpret your world?

What intellectual interest areas are you naturally drawn toward as a result of uncovering your pearls of wisdom?

If you have had a chance to "pass on" the wisdom that you have learned, when did you do so?

To whom did you pass the wisdom, and how did you choose to do so?

In what ways do you remind yourself of these valuable lessons? Do they come into play when you have important life decisions to make?

Personal Space

This is your opportunity to add your own thoughts and make notes.

_____

_____

_____

_____

_____

_____

_____

_____

_____

_____

_____

_____

_____

_____

ACTIVITY PURPOSE

To better understand how your intelligence is unique to you and your needs. ■

"   There are three kinds of intelligence: one kind understands things for itself, the other appreciates what others can understand, the third understands neither for itself nor through others. This first kind is excellent, the second good, and the third kind useless."

—*NICCOLO MACHIAVELLI*

activity 2 YOUR MULTIPLE INTELLIGENCES

Dr. Howard Gardner proposed a theory about people and their multiple types of intelligence. In this activity, you will rank Gardner's multiple intelligences for yourself and will learn about how they shape who you are.

Gardner suggested that intelligence measured on a single scale is too limiting to truly grasp how complicated intellect is. He proposed that people have nine types of intelligence. These areas of intelligence impact your ability to learn, or, more accurately, the ways in which you learn best.

THE STEP BY STEP

1   Read the descriptions that follow of Gardner's types of intelligence. Take a moment to ponder how important each is to you. Which area "fits" how you think, how you interpret the world?

2   Think about your preferred types of intelligence. Write down some skills you have that reinforce those intelligence areas. What are you able to do that makes you intelligent in this category?

3   After you have ranked the types of intelligence, create a list of how you personally utilize your top three intelligence areas. Create a second list with skills that you possess within that type of intelligence. A "favorites" list will emerge, identifying a group of things that you love to do. You will begin to understand how your unique intelligence type leads you to like these activities.

DISCOVERING YOUR MULTIPLE INTELLIGENCE PREFERENCES

Gardner's theory states that we all have multiple forms of intelligences that shape the way we learn and process information. Some forms of intelligence play a more dominant role in how each individual thinks. Listed next are Gardner's eight forms of intelligence; rank them in order of preference (1 = most preferred, 8 = least preferred). Remember that no individual intelligence is better than another, and you are intelligent to some degree in all areas.

_____ **LINGUISTIC INTELLIGENCE**

Linguistic Intelligence has to do with your grasp of words, whether spoken or written. People who excel in this area are generally proficient with writing and oration and have strong working vocabularies and pick up languages readily.

_____ **LOGICAL-MATHEMATICAL INTELLIGENCE**

Logical-mathematical intelligence has to do with numbers, logic, and abstract concepts. Those who are strong in this intelligence generally excel in mathematics and the computer fields and have a strong grasp of logic. Finding patterns and creating reason generally come easy to them.

_____ **SPATIAL INTELLIGENCE**

Spatial intelligence has to do with vision and spatial judgment. People strong in this area of intelligence are generally highly coordinated, have a strong technical recognition, can put things together easily, and have ability in art as well as tessellation (interrelation of shapes in a space, such as in loading a truck).

_____ **BODILY-KINESTHETIC INTELLIGENCE**

Bodily-kinesthetic intelligence has to do with muscular coordination, movement, and engaging in physically coordinated activity. People strong in this area of intelligence tend to be athletes or dancers. In addition, they learn better by doing things and interacting in a hands-on format.

_____ **MUSICAL INTELLIGENCE**

Musical intelligence has to do with hearing pitch and tone accurately and having a strong connection to music in general. Musically intelligent people tend to "work" to music and are effective in gleaning important information from lecture and other auditory learning methods.

_____ **INTERPERSONAL INTELLIGENCE**

Interpersonal intelligence has to do with a person's ability to interact with others. People strong in this intelligence tend to be extroverted, meaning they are more energized by being around other people than being alone. They feel comfortable around people because they are charismatic, convincing, and diplomatic. The interpersonal intellect tends to learn and perform best with groups of people.

_____ **INTRAPERSONAL INTELLIGENCE**

Intrapersonal intelligence has to do with self-understanding. People strong in this area tend to be introverted, meaning they prefer to think before they speak and prefer to get energy from time alone versus being in a large group setting. Often intrapersonal intellects house complex philosophies within them that are difficult for others to understand. People high in this form of intelligence tend to be drawn toward working in the clergy, in the field of psychology, and in other areas of human understanding and internal processing.

_____ **NATURALIST INTELLIGENCE**

Naturalist intelligence has to do with a person's connection to nature. People with a strong naturalist intelligence have a deep interest in the natural progression of life. These individuals are comfortable in situations where nature abounds.

In Figure 4–4, write down your top three intelligences. Then write down the skills that you have developed that reinforce your strengths in these three intelligence areas. For example, under "Intelligence Area," you choose "Musical Intelligence." Skills might include compose music, play piano and flute, understand beat and rhythm.

INTELLIGENCE AREA 1:
_____
_____
_____

INTELLIGENCE AREA 2:
_____
_____
_____

INTELLIGENCE AREA 3:
_____
_____
_____

FIGURE 4–4 My Top Three Intelligences and the Skills That Reinforce Them

Reflections

Now that you have developed your three intelligence areas, think about how they create the person who you are.

Stretch out your mind. How do your skills give you unique talents? How do you engage these talents?

How many of these things do you do on a regular basis?

Which activities are things you have wanted to do if only the opportunity would arise?

Which activities are ones that you have wished to do but have not yet had the opportunity to do?

How can you use these skills in your career or in planning your career path?

Personal Space

_____
_____
_____
_____
_____
_____
_____
_____
_____
_____
_____

activity 3 JOB INTERVIEWS FOR YOUR LIFE

Most likely, you have been involved in at least one job interview. This activity turns the table on the traditional interview. After answering some questions yourself, you will then use the same questions to interview others about you. Questions are provided, but you should add some of your own to better tailor the interview to who you are. What you will discover about yourself by comparing your answers to your peers will give you new insight into your cognitive identity.

COGNITIVE IDENTITY AND YOUR CAREER

It makes good sense that the areas in your life that you feel naturally drawn toward (intellectually) may connect to a career path. You are less likely to succeed in a career that contradicts your interests. How your intelligence works, the types of knowledge to which you are drawn, and the direction of your career are all tightly linked. By exploring your cognitive identity, your career choices will become clearer, and your values will more closely align with your chosen occupation.

You may be reading this as a student about to embark on a first career path. You may be coming from a very different direction, be it a career change or a desire to better understand how your identity enhances or challenges your work. When you create the additional questions for the following interview, consider what you already know about yourself. What makes your motivation for career success unique? How does your particular set of talents, experiences, and choices create a person that is unlike any other?

THE STEP BY STEP

1 Begin by reviewing the questions included in the following pages: The Job Interview for Your Life—Self-Interview (Figure 4–5) and The Job Interview for Your Life—Peer Interview (Figure 4–6).

2 You will notice in Figure 4–5 that there is space for you to add questions. Create questions that you would like to answer and have answered, and add them here.

3 After you have completed the *self*-interview, think of three people whom *you* would like to interview. Pick people from different areas of your life who know you well. Encourage them to answer honestly and with as many examples as possible, because this will give you a more defined idea of how *they* see your potential.

Utilizing the peer interview form (Figure 4–6), interview the three people.

ACTIVITY PURPOSE

To compare interviews of yourself and of your peers to discover your known and hidden abilities and values. ▣

"The best interviews—like the best biographies—should sing the strangeness and variety of the human race."

—*LYNN BARBER*

The Job Interview for Your Life—Self-Interview

Answer the following questions as if you were answering an interviewer's questions.

What would you list as your professional strength areas?

If you could envision yourself in any job, what would that job be?

What are three personal skills that you would like to utilize every day at work?

What types of work do you least like to do?

What strengths do you have in working with people?

If you could create an ideal working environment, what would it be?

What skills do you need to further develop to attain the kind of profession that you describe above?

Do you prefer to be in teams or alone when completing tasks and projects?

Add your questions here:

FIGURE 4–5

Job Interview for Your
Life—Self-Interview

The Job Interview for Your Life—Peer Interviews

What would you list as my professional strength areas?

Response 1:

Response 2:

Response 3:

If you could envision me in any job, what would that job be?

Response 1:

Response 2:

Response 3:

What are three personal skills that you think I would like to utilize every day at work?

Response 1:

Response 2:

Response 3:

What types of work do you think I least like to do?

Response 1:

Response 2:

Response 3:

FIGURE 4–6

Job Interview for Your Life—Peer Interview (*continued on next page*)

What strengths do you think I have in working with people?

Response 1:

Response 2:

Response 3:

If I could create an ideal working environment, what do you think it would be?

Response 1:

Response 2:

Response 3:

What skills do I need to further develop to attain the kind of profession that you describe above?

Response 1:

Response 2:

Response 3:

Do you think I prefer to be in teams or alone when completing tasks and projects?

Response 1:

Response 2:

Response 3:

FIGURE 4–6
continued

Add your questions here:

_____

Response 1:

_____

Response 2:

_____

Response 3:

_____

Response 1:

_____

Response 2:

_____

Response 3:

_____

Response 1:

_____

Response 2:

_____

Response 3:

_____

FIGURE 4–6
continued

Reflections

Now that you have interviewed three of your closest peers, colleagues, or family members, you are ready to compare their answers to yours. You may find many similarities between how you perceive yourself and how your peers evaluate your abilities. Utilize the following questions to process what you have written:

What are some themes that you began to discover as you read all of the responses?

Compare and contrast your responses to those you got from others.

How would you explain the differences between your answers and those of the people you interviewed?

How do the relationships that you have with each person impact the differences and similarities in the interviews?

What follow-up questions can you create based on what you've learned?

Which responses really represent you? Why?

What are some of the more surprising answers that you were given by your peers?

Personal Space

_____

_____

_____

_____

_____

_____

_____

_____

_____

_____

_____

_____

_____

_____

activity 4 | CAREER KALEIDOSCOPE

What is the right career path for you? This activity will bring skills and actions that you enjoy into sharp focus. You will discover how understanding what you like to do will lead you to a career that will bring you both satisfaction and success.

Part of picking the right kind of occupation is understanding how you like to spend your time at work. Many people find themselves in jobs that they plainly do not like. They are bored, crave challenge, and feel demotivated and underappreciated. More unfortunately, many of these people feel trapped.

This activity will help you prioritize your skills and interests. Not only will you gain a better understanding of your cognitive identity, but you will also find it easier to make career decisions. Your intellectual pursuits and the knowledge and wisdom you have acquired will impact your success on the job.

Your Personal Kaleidoscope

Kaleidoscopes are known for their ability to shape light into unique arrays of color and pattern. They are ever shifting and the viewer very rarely experiences the same images twice. This activity will ask you to bring together skills and tasks that you greatly enjoy in the workplace into new focus.

THE STEP BY STEP

1 Begin this activity by brainstorming a list of tasks that you enjoy or think you would enjoy in the workplace. Record them in Figure 4–7.

2 Now create a second list of skills that you most like to utilize when you are on the job. Record them in Figure 4–7.

3 On the provided kaleidoscope pattern (Figure 4–8), write a word from your two lists into each pattern space.

4 Once you have filled in as many pieces as you can, cut the kaleidoscope pattern into pieces and spread them out on a flat space.

5 Group the different skills into five theme areas that you can identify. Pick the top five tasks and skills that best fit each theme area.

6 Write this information on the worksheet provided in Figure 4–9.

ACTIVITY PURPOSE

To demonstrate how understanding your talents and skills can help you to better understand where your career path will lead you. ■

" People don't choose their careers; they are engulfed by them."

—UNKNOWN

In the following space, brainstorm a list of tasks that you enjoy in the workplace:

In the following space, brainstorm a list of skills that you most like to utilize when you are on the job.

FIGURE 4–7
Tasks That You Enjoy Performing
and Tasks That You Perform in
the Workplace

FIGURE 4–8 Your Career Kaleidoscope

Your Key Kaleidoscope Theme Areas

In the spaces provided below, write down your five career theme areas with the top five skills and tasks for each. Feel free to use the skills and tasks more than once if they fit under more than one theme area.

THEME AREA 1 TITLE: _____

    1. _____
    2. _____
    3. _____
    4. _____
    5. _____

THEME AREA 2 TITLE: _____

    1. _____
    2. _____
    3. _____
    4. _____
    5. _____

THEME AREA 3 TITLE: _____

    1. _____
    2. _____
    3. _____
    4. _____
    5. _____

THEME AREA 4 TITLE: _____

    1. _____
    2. _____
    3. _____
    4. _____
    5. _____

THEME AREA 5 TITLE: _____

    1. _____
    2. _____
    3. _____
    4. _____
    5. _____

FIGURE 4–9

Your Key Kaleidoscope
Theme Areas

Reflections

Now that you have created five career theme areas, you should have a better understanding of how your cognitive identity relates to your current or potential career. You have created five thematic considerations for the next time you evaluate a potential position for employment. You also now have tools that will help you to effectively evaluate whether or not your current job or career path fits your core being.

Which themes surprised you?

In what order would you rank the five theme areas, from most important to least?

What skills or tasks have you reused and why do you believe them to be so important to you?

How many of the developed theme areas fit your current career path or current job?

If you could create the ultimate job based on these skill areas, what would it look like?

Personal Space

_____

_____

_____

_____

_____

_____

_____

_____

_____

_____

_____

_____

COGNITIVE IDENTITY PERSONAL VISION PYRAMID

It is time now to make meaning out of the activities you have just completed. Using the Vision Pyramid, you will channel the energy within you to learn about your true identity.

1 What Is My Cognitive Identity?

As you progressed through the activities in this chapter, you no doubt began to notice consistent themes and ideas. Look through these activities and find 10 words, phrases, and ideas that are regularly occurring themes throughout your activity notes. Translate these themes into short statements to describe your cognitive identity. It is important to avoid making judgments at this point; they apply to core values in the following step. Simply pull out the observed themes. Write these 10 themes/statements here:

Example: *I am best suited to work in groups of people with whom I can share my perspectives.*

1. _____
2. _____
3. _____
4. _____
5. _____
6. _____
7. _____
8. _____
9. _____
10. _____

2 Develop Cognitive Core Values

Beginning with a solid sense of your identity is essential for developing meaningful core values. Core values are the principles, standards, or qualities that you consider worthwhile or desirable. Personal values form the criterion for evaluating what is important in your life. Look at the words, phrases, and ideas you listed in your core value statements. Look for specific themes. Do any of the themes merge? Spend some time looking at the 10 statements and find the patterns within. Condense the 10 words, phrases, and ideas listed above into five core values that fit how you feel you should live your life. Utilize the values list from Chapter 3 to help in the creation of this list. Write the five cognitive core values that you create here:

Example: *Variety in my intellectual tasks; being in an occupation that is outdoors*

1. _____
2. _____
3. _____
4. _____
5. _____

Create Specific Personal Cognitive Goals

Now it is time to create an action plan for your values! Creating effective personal goals fills the gap between who you are now and who you want to be. Review the core values that you have created and challenge yourself to develop specific actions (goals) for each one. What changes need to be made in your life to live by your core values? The best goals are S.M.A.R.T. (Specific, Measurable, Achievable, Realistic, and Timely). Begin by writing one personal goal for each core value here (you may wish to create more):

Example: *I will find three ways to bring variety into my intellectual and career pursuits by the end of the summer.*

1. _____
2. _____
3. _____
4. _____
5. _____

4 **Summarize Your Identity Area into a Cognitive Identity Mission Statement**

Your identity, five core values, and personal goals are the building blocks for a successful identity area mission statement. Mission statements provide a synopsis of the strategy behind a set of individual goals; they are a short written description of your purpose and direction. Missions should be easy to remember and should clarify where you want to go in life. In the personal space provided next, try to create a mission statement that summarizes your identity, values, and goals. Remember, mission statements are as unique as the individual creating them, and they don't need to be perfect!

Personal Space (My Cognitive Mission)

_____
_____
_____
_____
_____
_____
_____
_____
_____
_____

_____

_____

_____

_____

_____

_____

COGNITIVE IDENTITY ALTERNATIVE ROUTES

The activities offered in this chapter should serve as an effective starting point for learning more about your cognitive identity. The following sections provide numerous other resources and ideas that we would like to point you toward as you continue to explore who you are.

TAKE AN INTELLIGENCE TEST

There are a number of intelligence tests that you can take that give you useful information about your cognitive identity. Some measure select areas of intelligence, and others can be quite holistic in nature. You can consult career coaches, secondary schools, and college and university career centers for opportunities to take these assessments and learn about their meaning.

**For additional Web resources,
try searching with the following terms:**

IQ

Mensa

Wisdom

Tests

CREATE A SELF-DIRECTED LEARNING PROJECT

If there is an interest area that creates great curiosity within you, creating a self-directed learning project may help to quench that curiosity. To create one, you simply plan activities that will bring you new knowledge in your interest area. These projects can be ongoing (like this book) or may be more defined.

**For additional Web resources,
try searching with the following terms:**

Self-directed learning

Self-guided learning

Tutor

Encyclopedia

LEARN MORE ABOUT YOUR CAREER PATH

There are countless ways to learn about potential career paths. Most libraries have the Standard Occupational Classification (SOC) system, which contains a great deal of useful information about different careers. Resources are also available at most colleges and universities, at state and federal unemployment offices, and through employment and temporary services.

For additional Web resources, try searching with the following terms:

Career

Occupation

Jobs

Education

TAKE A CLASS, JOIN A WORKSHOP

A great way to fill up your curiosity fuel tank is to sign up for a course or workshop in your interest area. This may be a course at your local community college, vocational career center, or basic education center. Many of these courses are relatively inexpensive and offer you the benefit of learning with a group of peers. Alternatively, you can also take advantage of a number of online learning opportunities.

For additional Web resources, try searching with the following terms:

Online learning

Thomson Direct

Listserv

Blog

SELECTED BIBLIOGRAPHY

Gardner, H. (1993). *Frames of mind: The theory of multiple intelligence* (10th Anniversary ed.). New York: Basic Books.

The Cultural Identity Area

CALL IT A CLAN, CALL IT A NETWORK, CALL IT A TRIBE, CALL IT A FAMILY.

WHATEVER YOU CALL IT, WHOEVER YOU ARE, YOU NEED ONE.

■

—*JANE HOWARD, FROM* FAMILIES

CULTURAL IDENTITY

Cultural identity is a combination of your personal nature (genetics) and the different environments in which you have lived. It is both innate (born into you) and learned from the many people and places that you have experienced. You were born with a need for food; you didn't have to learn to be hungry. However, you did learn different ways of fulfilling that need. You learned when to eat, what to eat, and how to eat, among other things.

What's fascinating is that you have learned these cultural nuances from many, many different sources: parents, friends, school, church, TV, books, art, music, and so forth. In fact, you probably taught others and impacted culture too, knowingly or not. And in so doing, you also had an impact on your own culture. You may not even realize all the things you do that either reinforce or challenge cultural norms.

CULTURAL NORMS

What do we mean by cultural norms? These are the commonly accepted "rules" of society. For example, it is generally considered unacceptable to go out in public naked. Every time you leave the house wearing clothes, you support and reinforce this norm. A more severe example, hate crime, is supported and reinforced whenever someone witnesses it and does nothing. Taking a stand for

Your personal perspective of society, culture, and personal relationships.

The symbol used to signify cultural identity is a common symbol used in Native American cultures to represent ceremonial dances. These dances continue to be an important aspect of celebrating the relationships and values important in Native American culture. The symbol is used here to indicate celebration and pride in one's culture.

CULTURAL NORMS

are the commonly accepted rules of our society, the expectations that we have of each other within a given culture.

> " If you see in any given situation only what everybody else can see, you can be said to be so much a representative of your culture that you are a victim of it."
>
> —*S. I. HAYAKAWA*

> " Hell, there are no rules here—we're trying to accomplish something."
>
> —*THOMAS A. EDISON*

something you believe in is an important way in which you can express your cultural norms.

Your life is a constant cycle of affecting, learning, reinforcing, and internalizing cultural norms. Being born into this world was out of your control. You didn't get to pick your birth parents, your birth location, your race or gender, or your physical characteristics. On another level, there were *other* people who had some control of these things, but not you. For example, *you* didn't get to pick what food you ate as a baby, but *someone* did. *You* didn't get to pick where you grew up, but *someone* did. And on still another level are the things that you do personally have some control over, like who you associate with, what TV shows you watch, what books you read, and even the traditions you maintain. All of these things make up your cultural identity.

YOUR LIFE IS A CONSTANT CYCLE OF AFFECTING, LEARNING, REINFORCING,

AND INTERNALIZING CULTURAL NORMS.

That's right, you only have *some* control over the development of your cultural identity. Some of what you might think is free will or personal choice has already been programmed into you. There are some deep-seated reasons why you make the choices you do and why you believe the things you do. There's a reason why, for example, many middle-class Americans think that if you drive an expensive car, you must be successful. The accumulation of cultural norms creates stereotypes or assumptions about certain groups of people.

RECOGNIZING YOUR CULTURAL IDENTITY AND EXAMINING YOUR RELATIONSHIPS

Throughout our lives, we constantly refine who we are in the face of our culture. Recognizing your cultural identity is an important step in breaking the cycle of oppression in society and breaking free from the stereotypes and judgments of others. It is a crucial step in discovering your personal vision. You can continue your discovery in this chapter by exploring two things: who you are culturally and what you bring into your personal relationships.

ALL OF YOUR RELATIONSHIPS HELP TO INFLUENCE WHO YOU ARE.

All of your relationships help to influence who you are. There are those that you are born with (parents), those you are born into (family), and those you choose (friends, lovers). Relationships are so central to our lives that we frequently use them to introduce ourselves! For example, "Hi, I'm Aman's father, Sandeep . . ." or "Hi, I'm Shaelynn's supervisor." There is a reason why we use our key relationships to identify ourselves to others. These important relationships help to fundamentally shape how others see you and how you see the world.

If Sandeep is picking up Aman from daycare, but the teacher has never met Sandeep before, Sandeep would benefit by informing the teacher of his relationship to Aman. In doing so, Sandeep would be sharing part of his cultural identity.

The people who raised you, parents and caregivers, laid the foundation for your cultural identity. They typically establish your first definitions of right and wrong. Caregivers often give you the first examples of how you should relate with others. They typically provide you with the first tastes, sounds, and feelings you experience in life. They communicate important messages and beliefs to you by their behaviors, by their instructions, and in many other ways. They reinforce these messages repeatedly until you gain enough cognitive and emotional independence to decide if you want to adopt their beliefs, or instead look for new definitions. Those messages are also reinforced or challenged by other parts of your culture: religion, art, entertainment, media, and occupation.

Throughout the rest of your life, your beliefs get challenged, and you refine your beliefs based on what you learn from your life's journey. Those who raise you do not necessarily define you, but they certainly lay the foundation for your life. As you seek to change the masterpiece of your life, undoubtedly you must go back to investigate the foundation you were given during your formative years.

"
The bond that links your true family is not one of blood, but of respect and joy in each other's life. Rarely do members of one family grow up under the same roof."

—*RICHARD BACH, FROM* ILLUSIONS *(1977)*

AS YOU SEEK TO CHANGE THE MASTERPIECE OF YOUR LIFE, UNDOUBTEDLY

YOU MUST GO BACK TO INVESTIGATE THE FOUNDATION YOU WERE

GIVEN DURING YOUR FORMATIVE YEARS.

EXPLORING YOUR CULTURAL IDENTITY

Exploring cultural identity may be easier for some than for others. The concept of culture is laden with misleading stereotypes, negative connotations, and generalizations. Many would prefer to ignore key aspects of their cultural identity rather than face these stereotypes, connotations, and generalizations.

UNRAVELING YOUR CULTURE FROM THE NEGATIVE STEREOTYPES,

GENERALIZATIONS, AND CONNOTATIONS CAN REVEAL A GREAT DEAL

ABOUT WHO YOU ARE AND WHAT YOU ASPIRE TO BECOME.

Consider, for example, "white" American culture. Ask the average Caucasian American why he or she is proud to be white, and you will probably hear dead silence. Is this because there is no white culture? Of course there is white culture! Many white adults often tell us that they are uncomfortable talking about what it means to be white. What does it mean to be who you are? Unraveling your culture from the negative stereotypes, generalizations, and connotations can reveal a great deal about who you are and what you aspire to become. As an individual, you house your own personal culture. The diversity that lives within you not only connects you to like people but also separates you at times from people who are different. This is why members of a minority culture tend to group together when surrounded by the majority culture. We "clump" with people like us! So, what is the diversity to which we refer? Consider the following definitions of diversity. As you read these definitions, explore what areas are missing for you.

> *The harder you fight to hold on to specific assumptions, the more likely there's gold in letting go of them."*
>
> —*JOHN SEELEY BROWN*

DIVERSITY

Differences in race, ethnicity, creed, color, origin, geography

Differences in gender, sexual orientation, sexual identity

Differences in culture, heritage, upbringing, values

Differences in physical and mental ability, disability, age, appearance

Differences in socioeconomic class, wealth, poverty, privilege

Differences in religion, philosophy, ethics, morals

Differences in relationships

You have a full and unique culture that impacts who you are on a daily basis, whatever your racial or ethnic identity. As you work through the activities, remember that we define personal culture as a combination of your traditional cultural experiences and the relationships that you keep. Both of these areas define your cultural identity.

CULTURAL IDENTITY FOCUS POINTS AND ACTIVITIES

Your cultural identity is rooted in your personal perspective of society, culture, and personal relationships. It is the cumulative effect of upbringing, genetics, and your current world view.

As you complete the activities in this chapter, which are summarized in the following list, remember to keep track of reoccurring themes that present themselves to you. What types of values are you seeing repeatedly? How do your discoveries in these activities help you to understand yourself better? What topics reappear as areas that are intriguing? What are you learning about how you learn and how you best take in and store information?

Activity 1: License and Registration, Please. This activity will help you to break down your identity into the cultural groups with which you most closely identify. You are not an empty, mindless container to be filled with whatever your culture gives you. You make decisions about what things you accept and which you reject. You also have an active role in shaping your culture.

Activity 2: Food for Thought. One way to connect with the roots of your cultural identity is through food. This exercise will ask you to reflect on the foods of your youth and what correlations arise when you think about what these foods mean to you. Food can be a powerful memory tool, bringing you right back into the experience of your past. This may be an important discovery exercise for uncovering some things you may not have thought much about.

Activity 3: But Wait, There's More! We aren't expecting a cheesy infomercial from you, but this exercise will challenge you to describe your personality in a fun and safe way. You'll write an advertisement for yourself! In the process of reflecting on your advertisement, you'll identify some key aspects of your cultural identity and prioritize their importance and connection to you.

Activity 4: You Think What? This activity is a fun way to get your friends involved in your exploration! Don't worry, you won't be giving them a pile of homework, just a few simple questions. Their responses may be more valuable than you think. Here is where you'll "test" your self-perception with the perceptions of others who know you well. Are you being the authentic "you"?

To assist you in breaking down your identity into the cultural groups with which you most closely identify. ■

" ———————
      Who you are speaks so loudly that I can't hear what you are saying."

—*UNKNOWN*

activity I LICENSE AND REGISTRATION, PLEASE

In real life, our ID has become "proof" of several things: age, name, address, what we look like, and so forth. However, there are lots of "cards" we carry that we don't always show people. There are identities that are hidden from view, either purposefully or simply by their nature. For example, can you look at someone and know if they have a learning disability? Likely not. In fact, many people who have learning disabilities have developed such effective compensatory strategies that even their teachers or colleagues wouldn't be able to identify the disability—all the more reason why we should all allow others to identify themselves, rather than assigning them an identity based on our own assumptions.

In this activity, you get to lay your cards on the table and see what's what. Nobody is watching you or judging how you identify yourself; it's all about you. Be honest and open to what comes up in this exercise.

THE STEP BY STEP

1   Spend some time thinking about all of the different identity groups to which you belong. Remember that culture comes in many forms (language, race, ethnicity, relationships, socioeconomic status, geography, sexual orientation, gender, norms, activities, habits, etc.).

2   Now determine the elements of your cultural identity. Some examples of cultural identity elements are provided in Figure 5–1 to get you started. Write the elements of your personal cultural identity in the space provided in Figure 5–2. Try not to get stuck in the examples provided in Figure 5–1. They are not intended to be a comprehensive list, but merely a push to get you thinking.

3   Review the cultural identifiers that you selected. Next, in Figure 5–3, write down the personal characteristics that make you identify with each group. Is it because someone told you that you belong to that group, or is there something else? Why do you feel like you are part of this identity group? Maybe you don't feel a connection at all to a particular identity. That's good information too. Write it all down; now isn't the time to edit yourself. Get it out of your head and onto the page where you can see it first.

4   Now review what you've done so far, and select 5 to 10 areas with which you most strongly identify. Place an asterisk next to these.

5   In the space provided on the pages 80 through 82, name each identity and define what each means to you. What are the norms of your group, the shared values, the language, the traditions, the stereotypes, and the challenges?

6 For each identity that you claim, write a list of three reasons why you are proud to be part of that cultural group, and three stereotypes that others hold about that group.

AREA	EXAMPLES
Race	Asian, Black, Caucasian, Latino/a, etc.
Ethnicity	American, Native American, African American, European, Arabian, Indian, South East Asian, South American, etc.
Geographic origin	What country/state/region are you from? Are you a city person, a country person, suburban, rural, etc.?
Language	What is your primary language?
Gender	Male, female, transgendered, intersexed, etc.
Sexual orientation	Heterosexual, homosexual, gay, lesbian, bisexual, etc.
Socioeconomic	Wealthy, inheritance, middle class, etc.
Religious	Christian, Jewish, Buddhist, Muslim, Agnostic, Atheist, etc.
Political	Liberal, conservative, populist, libertarian, socialist, anarchist, democrat, republican, etc.
Age	In years? In sprit? As perceived by others? etc.
Ability	Physical, mental, intellectual, emotional, etc.
Habits	Smoker/nonsmoker, runner, book reader, drinker/nondrinker, musician, athlete, etc.

FIGURE 5–1
Example Elements of a Cultural Identity

1. _____ 9. _____
2. _____ 10. _____
3. _____ 11. _____
4. _____ 12. _____
5. _____ 13. _____
6. _____ 14. _____
7. _____ 15. _____
8. _____ 16. _____

FIGURE 5–2 Elements of My Cultural Identity

IDENTIFIER	PERSONAL CHARACTERISTICS THAT HELP YOU IDENTIFY WITH EACH IDENTIFIER
ex: West Coast	Born in California, laid back, vegeterian, long hair, surfer, etc.
ex: Male	Strong, vibrant, masculine, father, etc.

FIGURE 5–3 Identifiers and Personal Characteristics

CULTURAL IDENTITY

1: _____

Norms of This Group:

_____

_____

_____

_____

_____

Pride Points and Stereotypes of This Group:

_____

_____

_____

_____

_____

CULTURAL IDENTITY

2: _____

Norms of This Group:

_____

_____

_____

_____

_____

Pride Points and Stereotypes of This Group:

_____

_____

_____

_____

_____

CULTURAL IDENTITY

3: _____

Norms of This Group:

_____

_____

_____

_____

_____

Pride Points and Stereotypes of This Group:

_____

_____

_____

_____

_____

_____

CULTURAL IDENTITY

4: _____

Norms of This Group:

_____

_____

_____

_____

_____

Pride Points and Stereotypes of This Group:

_____

_____

_____

_____

_____

_____

CULTURAL IDENTITY

5: _____

Norms of This Group:

_____

_____

_____

_____

_____

_____

Pride Points and Stereotypes of This Group:

_____

_____

_____

_____

_____

_____

Reflections

Now that you have defined five of your core cultural identities, you have grounded yourself in your personal culture. You will now better understand how these cultural connections impact your identity as you answer the following questions:

How can you demonstrate your pride for each part of your cultural identity?

How can you challenge the assumptions of others based on negative stereotypes? How does your identity with these groups impact your life?

How has your identification with these core cultural identities changed over your lifetime?

Personal Space

This is your opportunity to add your own thoughts and make notes.

_____

_____

_____

_____

_____

_____

_____

_____

_____

_____

_____

_____

_____

_____

To reflect on the foods of your youth, and to understand what correlations arise when you think about what these foods mean to you. ■

> If more of us valued food and cheer and song above hoarded gold, it would be a merrier world."
>
> —J. R. R. TOLKIEN

activity 2 FOOD FOR THOUGHT

Food is an important part of cultural identity, and it's not just about the national origin of the food. Food can mark a memorable occasion, it can be part of a family tradition, it can be a reward for a valued accomplishment, or it can be what fuels you to do the things that are important to you. For this exercise, you will use the power of food to help you connect with your cultural identity. By remembering the foods that were important to you while growing up, you will spark some thoughts about the context and meaning of those foods.

THE STEP BY STEP

1 Think of the foods you grew up eating, the foods that maybe now remind you of home. Write down those foods along with what they mean to you. Some things to think about:

√ Who used to cook them for you?

√ Who taught you how to cook them, or who would you ask to teach you?

√ When did you eat them; was this a seasonal meal?

√ From what country or geographic area does that food come?

√ How do you identify with these foods?

√ What do they cause you to remember?

2 Now think about your top five favorite foods today. What cultural connections might these foods have? Where did you first eat them? What was the situation? Who were you with? How often do you still eat them?

3 Write the five most significant foods in your life in the space provided next. Write about the cultural significance that each food has for you. Then write about the cultural connection that this food creates for you from your past to your present.

Example

Your Favorite Food 1: Crepes

Cultural Significance:

When I was young, my grandmother used to make crepes for me with strawberries or syrup that she made. My grandmother often spoke French to me, and this reinforced my French culture.

Connection from Past to Present:

Whenever I eat crepes, I think of my grandmother and my French heritage. It has always caused me to want to rekindle my knowledge of the French language.

Your Favorite Food 1: _____

Cultural Significance:

_____

_____

_____

_____

_____

_____

Connection from Past to Present:

_____

_____

_____

_____

_____

_____

Your Favorite Food 2: _____

Cultural Significance:

_____

_____

_____

_____

_____

_____

Connection from Past to Present:

_____

_____

_____

_____

_____

_____

Your Favorite Food 3: _____

Cultural Significance:

_____

_____

_____

_____

_____

_____

Connection from Past to Present:

_____

_____

_____

_____

_____

_____

Your Favorite Food 4: _____

Cultural Significance:

_____

_____

_____

_____

_____

_____

Connection from Past to Present:

_____

_____

_____

_____

_____

_____

Your Favorite Food 5: _____

Cultural Significance:

_____

_____

_____

_____

_____

_____

Connection from Past to Present:

_____

_____

_____

_____

_____

_____

Reflections

Eating food is often a multisensory event. You have the obvious taste receptors that let you know whether the food is enjoyable or not. You then have your eyes, which appreciate the arrangement and color of the food. Your memory takes you to points in your past life when you ate food similar to that currently being tasted. It is that memory, and connection to your personal culture, that is being captured in this activity.

What is it that connects food to memory for you? Paying particular attention to your examples, why do you think the connection is so strong?

What are the common themes in your list?

Look for dishes that connect with each other. How do these foods connect to you and how you perceive your cultural identity?

Notice what kinds of food groups are missing from your list. What might this mean?

Personal Space

_____

_____

_____

_____

_____

_____

_____

_____

_____

_____

_____

_____

_____

_____

> Advertisements . . . contain the only truths to be relied on in a newspaper."
>
> —*THOMAS JEFFERSON*

activity 3 BUT WAIT, THERE'S MORE!

When an advertising agency develops a campaign to sell a product, its mission is to boil everything down to the most important selling points. Regardless of how creative or funny the advertisement is, it will not be effective in selling the product unless it is memorably clear about the product's most competitive selling points. It is not until a great deal of effort and debate has unearthed these most crucial aspects that advertisers even begin to develop a strategic way of communicating these core selling points.

You will be using the same strategy as advertisers, only you will be focusing on yourself, not some product on the shelves of the supermarket. But what if you were a product? What if you were in charge of selling yourself? What would you say? How would you determine what the core selling points were? What would you want the consumer to know and remember about you?

THE STEP BY STEP

1 Imagine that you are in a place where no one knows who you are. The expectation of this new place is that you place an ad in the personals section of the local newspaper. Everybody does it, and you have learned a lot about your new neighbors by reading through past issues. Your personal ad should describe *who* you are and not *what* you are. Here are some questions to start with (but don't limit yourself to these):

- Are you more extroverted (prefer to be around lots of people and get energized from that environment) or introverted (prefer smaller groups or alone time and feel tired after being in large groups)?

- Does your heart or your mind rule you more?

- Are you more of a "live in the moment" person or are you a dreamer?

- Do you generally prefer to plan in advance or do you prefer spontaneity in most situations?

- Are you a take-charge kind of person or someone who likes to take a more supportive role out of the limelight?

- What types of qualities do you look for in seeking out new relationships?

2 Use the space provided in Figure 5–4 to write your personal cultural advertisement, but limit yourself to 50 words or less. Feel free to be creative in your design, and be sure to include the vital aspects of your cultural identity. As with any personal ad, you can use abbreviations and phrases. Think about what things should go first. When you are done, reflect on *how* you decided what should be included and what should not. What things are missing that you wished you could have included?

FIGURE 5–4 Your Personal Cultural Advertisement

Reflections

In creating a personal advertisement about your cultural identity, you have somewhat forced yourself to figure out which cultural parts of you are most vital. This process of selecting a core cultural identity is important for understanding your personal vision.

What things did you list but ended up leaving out of your personal advertisement?

Were you surprised to find phrases and descriptions that you felt were vital that you may not have thought of as being cultural identity?

Show your personal advertisement to other people and find out what they think. Do they think it effectively describes who you are? What would they add or take away?

If you were reading other advertisements with the desire to find a friend or partner, what elements would you look for?

Personal Space

_____

_____

_____

_____

_____

_____

_____

_____

_____

_____

_____

_____

_____

_____

activity 4 **YOU THINK WHAT?**

Your relationships can say a lot about who you are. The people you choose to associate with often are a reflection of your interests, personality, work ethic, and core values, to name just a few things. This is not to say that everyone associates with people who are like them. On the contrary, we often associate with others who demonstrate some quality that we would like to have but feel like we don't currently have.

Your relationships say a great deal about your personal culture. Humans are naturally attracted to others who have values and priorities that are similar to theirs. Cultural identity is made up of not only your upbringing and cultural exposure, but also the people to whom you most closely relate and with whom you spend your time.

THE STEP BY STEP

1. List your five closest friends in Figure 5–5. Explain why they are your best friends. What unique qualities do they possess that you try to emulate in life? What similarities/differences do you have with these closest friends? Utilizing the envelope of values from the Value Sorter Activity in Chapter 3 may assist you.

2. In Figure 5–6, write down a list of 10 adjectives that describe you best. Then ask the five friends you listed in step 1 to make their own list of 10 adjectives that they think describe you best. If you want to get more feedback, you can also ask your closest family members, significant other, role models, mentors, coworkers, and so forth. Compare the lists and notice the similarities and differences. Do others see you the same way that you see yourself? What themes are emerging? Why do you think they exist?

ACTIVITY PURPOSE

To "test" your self-perception of cultural identity with the perceptions of others who know you well. ■

" Relationships of trust depend on our willingness to look not only to our own interests, but also the interests of others."

—*PETER FARQUHARSON*

NAME	WHY IS THIS PERSON YOUR FRIEND?	UNIQUE QUALITIES?	SIMILARITIES?	DIFFERENCES?

FIGURE 5–5 My Five Closest Friends

YOUR TEN ADJECTIVES	
YOUR FRIENDS' ADJECTIVES	
OTHERS' ADJECTIVES	
SIMILARITIES	
DIFFERENCES	
EMERGING THEMES?	

FIGURE 5–6 Friendly Reflections

Reflections

You have now had the opportunity to find out what your closest peers, family members, and colleagues think of you. In developing your cultural identity, it is crucial that you understand how your closest friends help to form your own sense of culture.

What are the core similarities that you have with your five closest friends?

What are some qualities that you hold the closest that you are not sensing in your friends?

How do some of your current friends help you to connect to past cultural influences?

Are there some aspects of your friendships that are so different that they sometimes create challenges?

Personal Space

_____
_____
_____
_____
_____
_____
_____
_____
_____
_____
_____
_____
_____
_____
_____
_____
_____

Personal Space

CULTURAL IDENTITY PERSONAL VISION PYRAMID

It is time now to make meaning out of the activities you have just completed. Using the Vision Pyramid, you will channel the energy within you to learn about your true identity.

1 **What Is My Cultural Identity?**

As you progressed through the activities in this chapter, you no doubt began to notice consistent themes and ideas. Look through these activities and find 10 words, phrases, and ideas that are regularly occurring themes throughout your activity notes. Translate these themes into short statements to describe your cultural identity. It is important to avoid making judgments at this point; they apply to core values in the following step. Simply pull out the observed themes. Write these 10 themes/statements here:

Example: *I believe that my culture is based on my Irish heritage.*

1. _____
2. _____
3. _____
4. _____
5. _____
6. _____
7. _____
8. _____
9. _____
10. _____

2 **Develop Cultural Core Values**

Beginning with a solid sense of your identity is essential for developing meaningful core values. Core values are the principles, standards, or qualities that you consider worthwhile or desirable. Personal values form the criterion for evaluating what is important in your life. Look at the words, phrases, and ideas you listed in your core value statements. Look for specific themes. Do any of the themes merge? Spend some time looking at the 10 statements and find the patterns within. Condense the 10 words, phrases, and ideas listed above into five core values that fit how you feel you should live your life. Utilize the values list from the Values Sorter in Chapter 3 to help in the creation of this list. Write the five cultural core values that you create here:

Example: *Family comes first in my life.*

1. _____
2. _____
3. _____
4. _____
5. _____

3 **Create Specific Personal Cultural Goals**

Now it is time to create an action plan for your values! Creating effective personal goals fills the gap between who you are now and who you want to be. Review the core values that you have created and challenge yourself to develop specific actions (goals) for each one. What changes need to be made in your life to live by your core values? Remember, the best goals are S.M.A.R.T. (Specific, Measurable, Achievable, Realistic, and Timely). Begin by writing one personal goal for each core value here (you may wish to create more):

Example: *I will spend at least three hours per week with my family beginning next week.*

1. _____
2. _____
3. _____
4. _____
5. _____

4 **Summarize Your Identity Area into a Cultural Identity Mission Statement**

Your identity, five core values, and personal goals are the building blocks for a successful identity area mission statement. Mission statements provide a synopsis of the strategy behind a set of individual goals; they are a short written description of your purpose and direction. Missions should be easy to remember and clarify where you want to go in life. In the personal space provided next, try to create a mission statement that summarizes your identity, values, and goals. Remember, mission statements are as unique as the individual creating them, and they don't need to be perfect!

Personal Space (My Cultural Mission)

_____
_____
_____
_____

_____

_____

_____

_____

_____

_____

_____

_____

_____

_____

_____

CULTURAL IDENTITY ALTERNATIVE ROUTES

The activities offered in this chapter should serve as an effective starting point for learning more about your cultural identity. The following sections provide numerous other resources and ideas that we would like to point you toward as you continue to explore who you are.

LEARN ABOUT DIVERSITY, MULTICULTURALISM, AND PRIVILEGE

The more you learn about the great variety of cultures, values, and perspectives, the greater you will begin to understand how you fit into the world. Reading about or attending workshops that help you to better understand the dynamics of difference will bring your cultural identity into sharper focus. It is vital that you understand any hidden prejudices so that they do not hinder your development.

For additional Web resources, try searching with the following terms:

Social justice

Diversity

Multiculturalism

Privilege

Cultural competence

UNDERSTAND YOUR RELATIONSHIPS

Part of your cultural identity has to do with your relationships. If you can understand the impact that your closest relationships have on you, it will bring you greater clarity. Many authors write specifically on improving interpersonal relationships; try to find their books to read. Meeting with a counselor/therapist who can help you to understand your interpersonal relationships can also be very insightful.

For additional Web resources, try searching with the following terms:

Relationship

Friendship

Kinship

Interpersonal

KNOW YOUR PERSONALITY

A number of personality inventories are available that can help you to better understand how your personality helps to shape your identity. Many counselors, both career and personal, can help interpret these instruments. There are also some very good books that contain personality inventories, explanations, and theory.

For additional Web resources, try searching with the following terms:

Personality type

Temperament

DISC Personality Profile

Myers-Briggs

Insights Discovery Personal Profile

The Big Five Personality

DISCOVER YOUR GENEALOGY

Researching your family history, or genealogy, can be an amazing process of self- and historical discovery. Understanding your cultural origins will help bring more definition to your cultural identity. Researching court records and family documents and even interviewing relatives can bring you great insight. You can also contact genealogists, who can assist you in discovering more about your family history.

For additional Web resources, try searching with the following terms:

Genealogy

Family tree

Ancestry

The Emotional Identity Area

NOTHING IS MORE IMPORTANT THAN EXPERIENCING YOUR FEELINGS. THEY ARE THE MOST SPONTANEOUS PART OF YOUR MAKEUP, THE MOST PRIMARY EXPRESSION OF YOUR AWARENESS AS IT RELATES TO THE WORLD.

■

DEEPAK CHOPRA, M.D., FROM TIMELESS BODY, AGELESS MIND

Your personal perspective of how your feelings guide who you are and how you see the world.

EMOTIONAL IDENTITY

This chapter is designed to help you identify, cope with, and harness your emotions. Emotions motivate (positively or negatively) your every action and they shape how you perceive others and how others see you. Getting to know the root of your emotions is critical to understanding who you are. Exploring your feelings will empower you to shape how you wish to feel in the future.

The symbol used to signify emotional identity is quite recognizable. Although this symbol is recognized now as a heart by most cultures, it was originally used in ancient apothecary work to represent ailments unrelated to the mind. It was regularly used to indicate an illness that was not identifiable in any parts of the physical body. It later became a pictorial representation for the human organ, the heart.

EMOTIONS MOTIVATE (POSITIVELY OR NEGATIVELY) YOUR EVERY ACTION AND THEY SHAPE HOW YOU PERCEIVE OTHERS AND HOW OTHERS SEE YOU.

WHERE DO EMOTIONS COME FROM?

Do your emotions come from the heart? On a conceptual level this is the common perception. The heart is the conceptual center of emotions, where humans build their capacity to love and hate, feel joy and sorrow, and experience happiness and anger. Having a big heart commonly means that you are caring. Being heartless is considered to be cruel or mean.

> " Anyone can become angry—that is easy. But to be angry with the right person, to the right degree, at the right time, for the right purpose, and the right way—this is not easy."
>
> —ARISTOTLE, FROM THE NICOMACHEAN ETHICS

Scientifically, your emotions are actually traced to a particular spot in your brain called the amygdala. The amygdala functions like an emotional memory bank. When something happens in your life, your amygdala triggers your limbic system to react based on an emotional memory. The accumulation of all of your emotional memories determines how you react to life's experiences. How you naturally react and express your emotions forms your emotional identity.

WHY IS EMOTIONAL IDENTITY IMPORTANT?

It is critical for you to understand how you naturally experience and express emotions. Emotions drive you to excel, to bring out your best, or to doubt and expose your greatest weaknesses. Emotions act as the accelerator and rudder for your thoughts and actions. Essentially, the patterns of how you feel over time shape who you are, how you interact with the world, and how you see yourself. There are three good reasons why you should get to know and direct your emotional identity:

1. Ignoring feelings creates outbursts, rage, depression, phobias, and confusion in our lives.

2. Harnessing emotions is empowering.

3. If you do not manage your emotions, others will.

REASON 1:
IGNORING FEELINGS CREATES A MISGUIDED LIFE

Some people believe that emotions should be hidden, especially negative emotions stemming from fear, anger, sadness, or disgust. Ignoring emotions like these is merely putting on a façade. Keep smiling when you're angry. Deny to others that you are sad by forcing yourself to be upbeat. The façade that you create to distract others from noticing your feelings merely alienates you and empowers the underlying emotion to grow in intensity. Feelings happen whether you want them to or not. Outburst, rage, depression, and/or phobias are the result of neglected emotions. Ignoring or subverting your emotion is a fast track to derailing your life. The accumulation of neglected emotions will dominate your time and mind, essentially holding you hostage to think, feel, and act in another way until the underlying emotion is acknowledged.

Self-awareness is the key to avoiding this spiral. Self-awareness is observing yourself and recognizing a feeling when it happens. To begin with, pay close attention to your physiological reactions when experiencing an emotion. Does your face contort when you are sad? What message is your body telling you? What is driving this feeling?

REASON 2:
HARNESSING EMOTIONS IS EMPOWERING

Once the roots of your emotions are uncovered, it is time to harness or redirect them for good purposes. What we are referring to is using your emotions in the service of a goal. Capture the emotional energy and channel it toward something useful. You can change the emotional pathways in your body to redirect, intensify, and express your emotional energy in different and better ways.

As the harnessing of emotions becomes more accomplished, you will gain the ability to control (in a healthy way) some of the emotions that come out of you as reactions. You will be able to better match a particular experience to emotions that you feel are appropriate.

REASON 3:
IF YOU DO NOT MANAGE YOUR
EMOTIONS, OTHERS WILL

People are under constant attack from others who wish to prey off the emotional energies flowing within them. Salespeople, politicians, coaches, and newscasters make a living on directing your emotions. They channel your emotions and motivate you to buy, vote, perform, and react in predetermined ways. For example, when you walk into a retail store, the music, lighting, color scheme, aromas, and customer service are all designed to help you feel comfortable, happy, and interested in their products. The purpose is for you to buy more. This strategy is incredibly effective.

Even people whom you believe you can trust can sometimes take advantage of you at vulnerable points. They may not be doing so intentionally, but many people take advantage of weak points to improve their positions. Many people are motivated by the positive emotion that results from helping others, and not necessarily by the desire to be selfless. Knowing your emotional identity will help you to stop taking advantage of others and to recognize when others are pushing your buttons.

> Cherish your own emotions and never undervalue them."
>
> —*ROBERT HENRI*

EMOTIONAL IDENTITY FOCAL POINTS
AND ACTIVITIES

Your emotional identity is rooted in how your feelings inform you and guide you.

As you complete the activities in this chapter, which are summarized in the following list, remember to keep track of reoccurring themes that present themselves to you. What types of values are you seeing repeatedly? How do your discoveries in these activities help you to understand yourself better? What topics reappear as areas that are intriguing? What are you learning about how you learn and how you best take in and store information?

Activity 1: The Anatomy of Emotions. Your body and your mind are intimately connected. When you feel something strongly, there is often a definite physical manifestation of that emotion. You will learn to use the physical clues in your body to discover your emotional state.

Activity 2: The Emotion Superhighway. Happy, sad, mad, afraid, bored, nervous, anxious, curious—there are millions of feelings that shape who we are every second of every day. This activity is designed to help simplify and clarify your emotions by discovering the eight primary emotions that form the basis for all other emotions in your life: anger, fear, joy/happiness, sadness, love/acceptance, disgust, surprise, and interest/curiosity. Think of these eight primary emotions as a rotary with incoming traffic from numerous highways. Combining any or all of these eight incoming emotions creates an infinite number of possible emotions. You will get a chance to break down the important emotions at play in your life to find out how much and when you are truly ruled by your heart.

Activity 3: Your Kid Fears and Joys. Fear is an emotion that we all know well. This activity will help you to rediscover the fears and joys that you experienced as a child. You will explore how they impact your life today.

Activity 4: Games People Play. We all play emotional games with the people we know, consciously or subconsciously. Usually these games keep us more emotionally safe in the moment, but they tend to complicate our long-term lives and relationships. Once you understand some of these games, you will be able to better control when and how you use them.

activity 1 **THE ANATOMY OF EMOTIONS**

It may seem at first glance that your feelings are quite obvious. Recognizing the origins of your emotions may be easy for some people, but for many, emotions are elusive and mysterious. The connection between heart and mind is short and well traveled. Your heart and mind work together to identify feelings and choose appropriate reactions. However, it may be all too easy to recall a time when your feelings got the best of you and you said or did something regrettable.

THE CONNECTION BETWEEN HEART AND MIND IS SHORT AND WELL TRAVELED.

In this exercise we will empower you to observe and recognize feelings when they happen. You will learn to use the physical clues in your body to better understand your emotional state.

Let's begin with exploring the roots of emotions. The Latin root of *emotion* is *motere*, which means "to move," plus a prefix "e," which means "move away." Thus the original intention of the word *emotion* was an impulse to act by moving away. For example, the natural impulse to fear is to move away from danger. An impulse is a form of energy in your body. It is helpful to think of emotions as multiple forms of energy that move through your body. Each emotion is a slightly different form of energy and, therefore, needs to be understood and processed differently. Think of your body as a channel for the energy, much like a riverbed acts as a channel for water. When you feel an emotion, it is the sensation of that energy moving through your body. Emotions will be felt in different places in your body. Because every person's body is different, the channels for emotions vary from person to person.

Scientists have been able to track physiological reactions in the body to certain emotions. Anger causes blood to flow to the hands, making it easier to grasp a weapon or strike out. The body produces an excess of adrenaline to increase strength and agility. Fear causes blood to flow to skeletal muscles, such as those in the legs, causing your face to go pale. Happiness causes increased brain activity, blocking out negative feelings. The limbic system sends a collection of hormones throughout the body that bring a sense of pleasure. These physiological reactions are generalized for most people. Does your face turn red when you are mad? Do your palms sweat when you are nervous? Does your heart beat slowly when you are feeling sad? Knowing how your body reacts is a helpful tool in identifying emotions.

THE STEP BY STEP

This exercise is designed to help you map out where and how you feel certain emotions. Do you clutch your heart when you are feeling loved? Does your face turn bright red and feel hot when you're mad? Do you feel lethargic when you're sad? These are stereotypical bodily reactions to emotions. Think beyond these stereotypes. Where do you feel jealousy, confusion, frustration, romantic love versus family love? No two bodies are alike.

 Picture your body as a river channel. Imagine your emotions moving through your body like water.

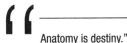

2 During the next several days spend some time thinking about different sensations in your body when you feel sad, mad, scared, curious, happy, and/or loved. Where do you feel each of these emotions? Take notes on these physical manifestations of your emotions.

EXAMPLE:

My body feels chills when I see my boss.

I get a headache when I feel stressed.

I feel light-headed when I kiss my partner.

My armpits perspire when I get nervous.

3 Figure 6–1 shows a diagram of a body. Label this figure with your emotions; draw an arrow to the parts of the body that accompany each of them.

4 Add notes in the margin. The key to this exercise is mapping out how your body reacts to certain emotions. This will help you read your body and more quickly diagnose what you are feeling.

FIGURE 6–1
Where I Feel My Emotions

Reflections

Now that you have "mapped" your emotions as they relate to the physical responses in your body, take some time to process how this impacts you.

Emotional energy will flow, pool, and stir through your body. In keeping with the water metaphor, how fast is the water (emotion/energy) moving? Where is it going? Where does the water collect?

Describe the sensation in your gut, heart, head, or hands that connects with the emotions you have recorded. Does your body feel energized, lethargic, off balance, hot/cold, and so forth?

How do the physical manifestations of your emotions enhance you or hold you back? Are there ways that you could use this knowledge to your advantage?

Personal Space

This is your opportunity to add your own thoughts and make notes.

_____

_____

_____

_____

_____

_____

_____

_____

_____

_____

_____

_____

_____

_____

_____

To think about how your emotions interplay with each other to create unique reactions and to find out how much and when you are truly ruled by your heart. ■

"

People decide far more problems by hate, love, lust, rage, sorrow, joy, hope, fear, illusion, or some other inward emotion, than by reality, authority, any legal standard, judicial precedent, or statute."

—*CICERO*

activity 2   **THE EMOTION SUPERHIGHWAY**

Happy, sad, mad, afraid, bored, nervous, anxious, curious—there are millions of feelings that shape who we are every second of every day. Thus, the task of exploring your emotions is infinitely complex. Modern American psychology has independently studied the hundreds of emotions that people experience and found that all emotions stem from eight primary emotions. These emotions, which can exist at various levels of intensity, are anger, fear, joy/happiness, sadness, love/acceptance, disgust, surprise, and interest/curiosity. Think of these eight primary emotions as a rotary with incoming traffic from numerous highways. Combining any or all of these eight incoming emotions creates an infinite number of possible emotions. For example, feeling nervous can be the combination of fear and interest. Adding to the intensity of interest changes the feeling to anticipation.

THE STEP BY STEP

1   Figure 6–2 shows an "emotion superhighway." Notice how the rotary has eight incoming highways representing the eight primary emotions.

2   As these emotions come together into the center, they overlap and cross each other. Write in places where these emotions combine for you.

3   Figure 6–3 is a worksheet that you can use to more deeply define how these combinations of emotion impact and influence you.

YOUR EMOTIONAL SUPERHIGHWAY

This activity is about expanding your understanding of your emotional superhighway. Imagine a large superhighway with traffic (emotions) coming in from eight separate directions. When two or more emotions combine, a new secondary or tertiary emotion is created. See how many emotions you can combine at various levels of intensity to expand the understanding of your emotional superhighway.

For Example:

◉ Love and sadness may combine to create *jealousy*. Intensifying love may change the feeling to *heartache*.

◉ Fear and joy may intersect to form the kind of *curiosity* felt when watching a gruesome horror movie.

◉ Anger and interest may intersect to create a *passion* for solving frustrating problems. Intensifying anger with interest may change the feeling to create *hatred*.

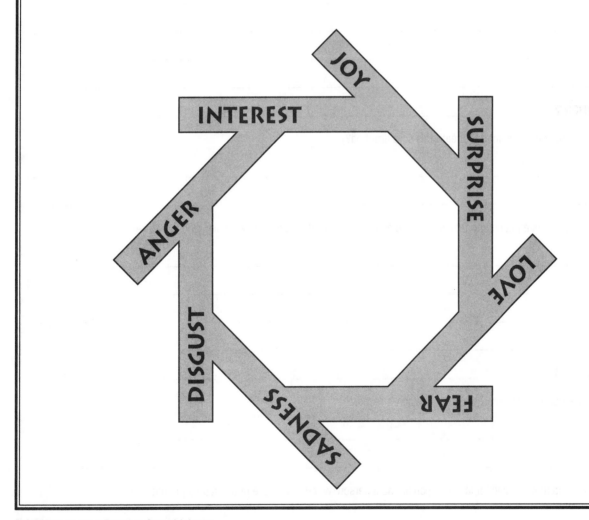

FIGURE 6–2 Your Emotion Superhighway

Understand Your Physical Emotions

On this worksheet, take some time to better understand the emotions that you have identified. Begin by selecting the five core emotions that play the most important roles in your life.

CORE EMOTION 1: _____

What primary emotions combined to create this core emotion?

_____

_____

In what ways does this emotion impact who you are as a person, whether positive or challenging in nature?

_____

_____

_____

_____

CORE EMOTION 2: _____

What primary emotions combined to create this core emotion?

_____

_____

In what ways does this emotion impact who you are as a person, whether positive or challenging in nature?

_____

_____

_____

_____

CORE EMOTION 3: _____

What primary emotions combined to create this core emotion?

_____

_____

In what ways does this emotion impact who you are as a person, whether positive or challenging in nature?

_____

_____

_____

_____

FIGURE 6–3 Understanding the Crossroads (*continued on next page*)

CORE EMOTION 4: _____

What primary emotions combined to create this core emotion?

_____

_____

In what ways does this emotion impact who you are as a person, whether positive or challenging in nature?

_____

_____

_____

_____

CORE EMOTION 5: _____

What primary emotions combined to create this core emotion?

_____

_____

In what ways does this emotion impact who you are as a person, whether positive or challenging in nature?

_____

_____

_____

_____

FIGURE 6–3 *continued*

Reflections

Now that you have discovered five core emotions that have a strong impact on your everyday existence, think about the following questions to more deeply understand the impact of this new information:

Which of the primary emotions do you feel the most frequently? Which emotions are you less likely to experience?

For which core emotions did you struggle to determine the root emotions? Did you find at times that all or too many of the core emotions were combinations of other emotions?

Which core emotions were the easiest for you to create? Are these emotions helpful or harmful to you?

How do your core emotions tie into your personal identity?

Personal Space

_____

_____

_____

_____

_____

_____

_____

_____

_____

_____

_____

_____

_____

_____

_____

activity 3 YOUR KID FEARS AND JOYS

ACTIVITY PURPOSE

To understand how the fears that you developed as a child continue to impact your emotional identity. ■

Fear of the dark, monsters under your bed, "breaking your mother's back if you step on a crack"—these are the kinds of fears that we developed as children. In their song "Kid Fears," Amy Ray and Emily Saliers from the Indigo Girls sing about the kid fears that we develop and how they follow us into our adulthood.

What would you give to live with only your simple kid fears? As with many good poetic lyrics, the Indigo Girls intended a dual meaning with the lyrics of "Kid Fears." Many of our deepest fears (and joys) stem from experiences from our childhood. Adult abandonment, shame, and codependence issues are often products of childhood scars.

How you interpret and express love, show interest, and find happiness is deeply seated in your childhood memories. Do you have fears/joys as an adult that trace back to your childhood? Do you ever find that a simple thing that most people find harmless triggers emotional reactions within you (positively or negatively)? Beginning early in childhood, we collect emotional memories that have an evolutionary effect on shaping who we are. How you feel emotions forms an essential part of who you are. Likewise, how you learn to express, interpret, and bury emotions also is important in determining who you are. Now, what would you give for your kid fears?

> " Are you on fire . . . from the years. . . . What would you give for your kid fears?"
>
> —*INDIGO GIRLS, FROM "KID FEARS"*

BEGINNING EARLY IN CHILDHOOD, WE COLLECT EMOTIONAL MEMORIES THAT

HAVE AN EVOLUTIONARY EFFECT ON SHAPING WHO WE ARE EMOTIONALLY.

This activity is designed to help you get back in touch with the emotional reactions you learned and experienced when you were a child. You will recall your childhood emotions and think about them in light of the emotions you experience today as an adult. Some emotions may seem trivial compared to the challenges you face now. This will give you perspective about the changes you have undergone. You may find that other emotions are just as valid today as they were when you were a kid. These realizations are critical to helping you understand why you feel the way you do at certain times.

Feelings are, by nature, not rational. They are difficult to understand and vary from person to person. It is important that you get in touch with your emotions and feel comfortable building your own understanding of your emotions. This will help you discover for yourself the influence your emotions have on crafting who you are and who you can be.

THE STEP BY STEP

We all have childhood memories of emotional events that stick with us. Think back to your earliest memories of fear.

 1 Close your eyes and try to visualize a memory of your greatest fears and greatest joys as a child. This is best done when you have time and space to think and be alone.

2 Journal your thoughts on a separate piece of paper by describing what comes to your mind. Write down what your first thoughts are, not what you think you *should* write.

3 Now move to Figure 6–4. Starting with your right hand, on the right side of the page, describe the facts. Where were you? What was happening? Who was with you? Using your right hand will better connect you with the rational side of your brain. With your left hand, writing on the left side of the page, pull from the creative/imaginative side of your brain. Express how you felt emotionally and physically. This activity will work with right- and left-handed writers. Pay close attention to sensations in your body: scents, sounds, colors, shapes. Try not to judge your emotions. Use as much space as you need. There is no structure, format, or rules to this expression. Stop when you feel like stopping.

Note: It does not matter which hand is most dominant for writing purposes.

Kid Fears	
FEELINGS	**FACTS**

FIGURE 6–4 My Kid Fears and Joys

Reflections

Now that you have remembered and expressed your kid fears, consider what they really mean to you.

How do they continue to impact your day-to-day experiences?

Have you felt the emotions that you described recently? When, where, and why?

How often do you feel this way and what seems to be the trigger(s)?

What options do you have to express this feeling in the future?

What do you do when you feel this way? Do you try to suppress your emotional outlet, or do you let things flow?

Have these joys or fears led to positive actions in your life? Negative?

What are the three most powerful kid emotions you experienced most recently?

Personal Space

_____

_____

_____

_____

_____

_____

_____

_____

_____

_____

_____

_____

_____

_____

_____

To understand how the inter-personal games that you play impact the emotions that you share with others. ■

> " ———————
> There can be no transform-ing of darkness into light and of apathy into movement without emotion."
>
> —CARL JUNG, SWISS PSYCHIATRIST, 1875–1961

activity 4 GAMES PEOPLE PLAY

Emotions can be contagious. For example, fear and joy are two very trans-mittable emotions—think of a time when people around you are either extremely joyful or in fear; you can almost feel the emotion come out of them and into you. People sometimes temporarily hijack your emotions to motivate you in intentional ways; they play games with you.

A larger-scale example of this hijacking can be seen on television when the media speaks of the "threat of terrorism." This specific threat impacts one of your most primary emotions: fear. Fear motivates you to be more cautious, thus reducing the risk of attack and harm. Individuals can motivate these kinds of emotional responses as well. You may learn you do it to others.

This activity will ask you to think about the games that you play with people (and in turn the ones they play with you). You will probably find yourself embarrassed at times, because while we all know that these games are potentially damaging, we continue to play them. Most of the time we do so because engag-ing in these games protects our true emotions. In essence, they are an easy way out of complicated situations.

THE STEP BY STEP

Eight "games people play" to influence others by tapping into their emo-tions are given next. Your ability to identify these games, figure out the "game plan," and alter the playing field to create a win–win situation will significantly impact your success in difficult social settings. Before you begin, realize that we all play these games; the trick is to realize the impact that they are having on our emotional identity.

1. In the following pages, you will be given a brief description of each of the eight games that people play. Write down exam-ples that you know of where you play the given game.

2. The second part of this activity is to recognize the game plan that exists and to dissect why you are engaging in the behavior.

3. Now that you understand why you do it, what can you do to change your behavior? Write down strategies for change!

The Blame Game

The Blame Game happens when you shift blame to others rather than tak-ing personal responsibility for a given situation/mistake. You blame a particular person or a whole group of people. It may also mean that you blame a system or something less tangible for your own failure.

Example

I was late in turning in the monthly report, but instead of taking re-sponsibility I blamed the computer systems in the office and my ad-ministrative assistant for not reminding me.

OR

I was not able to plan my mother's birthday party; instead of taking responsibility I blamed the caterer for not being able to do the job quickly enough, and I also blamed the restaurant for not having the availability I needed.

Write down examples of when you have used the Blame Game:

_____

_____

_____

_____

_____

_____

_____

_____

_____ **THE GAME PLAN**

You are casting away unwanted feelings (anger, disgust, fear, or sadness) and projecting them on another person or thing through blame.

- What are the unwanted feelings that you are trying to avoid?

- What can you do to better cope with these feelings without blaming someone else?

_____

_____

_____

_____

_____

_____

_____

_____

_____ **THE WIN-WIN SITUATION**

Stop shifting blame to others, cope with the emotion that you are trying to avoid, and take responsibility for your actions.

- How can you harness the negative emotional energy to find a solution that benefits you and allows you to take responsibility?

- What makes it so attractive to blame others, and how can that be reduced?

_____

_____

_____

_____

_____

_____

_____

_____

The Comparing Game

The Comparing Game happens when you compare yourself to others to show superiority over them. You may be doing this in order to make yourself feel better about your personal faults that you would rather not consider. You play this game so that you can bring another person down in order to inflate your personal being.

Example

You know that you need to gain better speaking skills, and instead of acknowledging that, you spend your time thinking of the people around you who have less skill than you.

OR

You mismanage your money, and instead of fixing the problem you spend time comparing yourself to others who are worse off than you.

Write down examples of when you have used the Comparing Game:

_____

_____

_____

_____

_____

_____

_____

_____

_____

THE GAME PLAN

You have an unmet esteem need/want stemming from a perceived lack of importance or value which motivates you to put others down through comparison.

- What is the unmet esteem need/want? What is the root insecurity?
- How can you feel more important/powerful in this situation?

_____

_____

_____

_____

_____

_____

_____

_____

_____ THE WIN-WIN SITUATION

Avoid the need to compare yourself to others and instead provide support to others.

- What part of your emotional identity is causing you to make these excuses by comparing?
- How can you avoid the temptation to compare yourself to others and make more effective change in your life?

_____

_____

_____

_____

_____

_____

_____

_____

The Competition Game

The Competition Game happens when you compete with others to assert dominance where dominance is not necessary or helpful. There is a part of your emotional identity that makes you want to win even at the expense of others.

Example

You are assigned the same tasks as others on your team. Instead of focusing on completing your tasks, you spend energy finding ways to derail others from completing their tasks.

OR

You are in a social setting and feel a sense of intimidation about another person that causes you to contradict everything the person is saying with your own perspective.

Write down examples of when you have used the Competition Game:

_____

_____

_____

_____

_____

_____

_____

_____

_____ THE GAME PLAN

You have an unmet emotional need for recognition that is not being satiated. This may be because you are craving additional attention or because you feel that you deserve more recognition than you are receiving.

◼ Why do you feel motivated to feel better at the expense of others?

◼ How can you cope with the loss of that need?

_____

_____

_____

_____

_____

_____

_____

_____ THE WIN–WIN SITUATION

Competing with others leads to a winner/loser mentality. Instead, provide validation for what others may be suggesting. Learn to separate your own emotional needs from those that you wish to impose on others.

◼ How can you resist competing with others and instead support them without feeling defeated?

_____

_____

_____

_____
_____
_____
_____
_____

The Denial Game

The Denial Game happens when you have avoided acknowledging the obvious problems at hand either consciously or subconsciously. Basically, you are ignoring the problem by denying its existence.

Example

You are constantly arriving late for a meeting or a class, and instead of creating better strategies for being on time, you ignore the feedback from others.

OR

You have been feeling ill for some time, but instead of going to a doctor, you figure it is just some sort of odd flu or something.

Write down examples of when you have used the Denial Game:

_____
_____
_____
_____
_____
_____
_____

_____ **THE GAME PLAN**

You are avoiding an unwanted, uncomfortable reality or fear by denying what is really happening for a safer, alternative reality.

■ What is the loss that you would feel by accepting the true situation?

■ How can you create ways to cope with the frustrations of the true emotion?

_____
_____
_____
_____
_____
_____

_____   **THE WIN–WIN SITUATION**

Create an acceptance and understanding of your emotional identity so that you can accept the truth and your responsibility and thus maintain your integrity.

■ How can you prepare yourself for living out the real responses to a challenging situation rather than denying?

_____

_____

_____

_____

_____

_____

_____

_____

The Expert Game

The Expert Game happens when you act as the "know-it-all" expert and deny others the opportunity to be a part of the answer. This game makes you seem arrogant and inflexible.

Example

You have completed a task a number of times, and someone new to the task suggests a new strategy. Instead of listening to that person's suggestion, you assert your expert status and overrule.

OR

Your significant other tells you that there is a different way to get to a restaurant that you both like, but instead of hearing the new way, you refer to the fact that you have been there many times and that you know the best way.

Write down examples of when you have used the Expert Game:

_____

_____

_____

_____

_____

_____

_____

_____

_____   **THE GAME PLAN**

You are avoiding an unwanted feeling by not listening to the suggestions of others. You may be feeling defensive or maybe you are being overconfident in the situation.

■ What feeling are you blocking by being the "know-it-all"? What is being threatened?

■ How would you feel in the situation if you were not the expert?

_____

_____

_____

_____

_____

_____

_____

_____

_____   **THE WIN-WIN SITUATION**

Understand that blocking others' perspective reduces input and makes you look like an inflexible person. Also understand that there are underlying reasons why you want to maintain control in the situation. Why is that?

■ What is it about the given situation that makes you want to overstep others and assert your answers?

■ Is a relationship issue with someone keeping you from accepting your emotions?

■ How can you clearly state your perspective and at the same time allow others to give input?

_____

_____

_____

_____

_____

_____

_____

_____

The Assumption Game

The Assumption Game happens when you assume something about people or situations without asking questions to find out what is really occurring. Assumptions quickly turn into prejudices and stereotyping.

Example

You are about to select people for a team, and instead of selecting your teammates based on their abilities, you select people whom you feel are most like you and will not "rock the boat."

OR

You are meeting people for a social engagement and your friend Mary is late again. Instead of asking what happened, you just assume that since she is a woman, she probably spent too much time getting ready.

Write down examples of when you have used the Assumption Game:

_____

_____

_____

_____

_____

_____

_____

_____

_____ **THE GAME PLAN**

You jump to conclusions in a given situation as a shortcut to avoid the emotions that may come from knowing the truth. You pigeon-hole people into categories that allow you to create shortcuts in how you see others.

- What are the emotions that you are hiding from that cause you to make assumptions about the person? Do you know too little about them and just do not want to know more?

- What are your prejudices? Do you make any assumptions about groups of people that are unfair?

_____

_____

_____

_____

_____

_____

_____

_____   **THE WIN-WIN SITUATION**

You make assumptions because you are uncomfortable with the truth that exists within the situation or yourself. You need to consider each person and situation to be unique.

- ◙ What biases and prejudices may be at work that keep you from seeking the truth?

- ◙ How can you erase the biases that you have so that you are emotionally prepared to accept every situation as a new one?

_____

_____

_____

_____

_____

_____

_____

_____

Living-in-the-Past Game

The Living-in-the-Past Game happens when you forgo what is happening in the present for things that have worked in the past. Usually, you do this because the past way is the way it has always been done and that is what is most comfortable to you.

Example

You are given the task of changing a procedure at your workplace. Your manager has given you three valid reasons why the procedure needs to change. After thinking about it for a long time, you go back to your manager and instead of supporting the change, you attempt to invalidate her reasons, thereby making the changes unnecessary.

OR

You arrive at your favorite restaurant and order your favorite meal. When your meal comes to you, you notice that it has been prepared differently. The server tells you that a new chef has been hired who has changed some of the menu items. Instead of trying the new version of your favorite meal, you decide to leave and not return to the restaurant.

Write down examples of when you have used the Living-in-the-Past Game:

_____

_____

_____

_____

_____

_____

_____

_____

_____ THE GAME PLAN

Change is difficult, and your emotional identity often creates a need to maintain systems that you believe have always worked. The fear of change drives you to refuse acknowledging the need for change.

- ▣ What are you afraid will happen if you allow change to occur?
- ▣ Being reasonable, the past may be the safest option, but is it the best?

_____

_____

_____

_____

_____

_____

_____

_____ THE WIN–WIN SITUATION

When you live in the present and accept the needs of the now, you are better able to make sound decisions. Old solutions do not always fit.

- ▣ What emotional connections exist within your desires to live in the past?
- ▣ How much of your need to live in the past is finding an easy way out of a difficult challenge?

_____

_____

_____

_____

_____

_____

_____

The Passive Aggressive Game

The Passive Aggressive Game happens when speech and actions send opposing messages. In some situations, the level of vulnerability is so high that you are not comfortable sharing your true reactions. Instead you maintain the expected response and then vent that frustration to others at a later time and under safer circumstances.

Example

You are driving in traffic and someone cuts you off. Just as you are about to give the person a piece of your mind, you notice that she looks pretty threatening. You decide to give her a gentle wave and a smile. Later when you get home, you yell at your dog for whimpering at the door.

OR

You have been working on your computer for hours on a project when there is a system crash and you lose a third of your work. Your roommate walks in about a half hour later and you angrily confront him about not putting his dishes into the dishwasher that morning.

Write down examples of when you have used the Passive Aggressive Game:

_____

_____

_____

_____

_____

_____

_____

_____

_____ THE GAME PLAN

There are many situations in which responding emotionally to the true core of your frustration is either impossible or too risky. You then let loose your emotional fury at a safer target. Many abusive relationships work this way. The partner becomes the victim to an abuser who has external frustrations and then takes them out on the safe partner.

- When playing the Passive Aggressive Game, what keeps you from confronting the source?

- Why do you let your frustrations build to sometimes double or triple the anger and then dump it on someone else? Why did you choose your particular target?

_____

_____

_____

_____

_____

_____

_____

_____

_____   **THE WIN-WIN SITUATION**

It is vital that you begin to notice on whom you dump your frustration. Your emotional identity will become more effective when you can recognize what you are doing. Learn to appropriately confront and react to situations, and then let them go.

- Who are the people you dump on, and how will you stop this behavior?

- What are some safe ways that you can use up your aggressive emotions without aiming them at an innocent victim?

_____

_____

_____

_____

_____

_____

_____

_____

Reflections

Now that you have reviewed the games that people play, it is time to think a bit about how these games impact your emotional identity. Remember that everyone plays these games, and the trick is for you to recognize which ones you most frequently utilize and how that impacts who you are.

Were there certain games that you discovered you play more than others? Why do you think this is?

Were you able to discover some coping mechanisms that you can use to stop yourself from playing the games? What are they and how can you use them?

What is the potential for understanding when others are using these games against you? What techniques can you use to tell the person what is happening or to challenge his or her thinking?

Personal Space

_____
_____
_____
_____
_____
_____
_____
_____
_____
_____
_____
_____
_____
_____
_____
_____

EMOTIONAL IDENTITY PERSONAL VISION PYRAMID

It is time now to make meaning out of the activities you have just completed. Using the Vision Pyramid, you will channel the energy within you to learn about your true identity.

 What Is My Emotional Identity?

As you progressed through the activities in this chapter, you no doubt began to notice consistent themes and ideas. Look through these activities and find 10 words, phrases, and ideas that are regularly occurring themes throughout your activity notes. Translate these themes into short statements to describe your emotional identity. It is important to avoid making judgments at this point; they apply to core values in the following step. Simply pull out the observed themes. Write these 10 themes/statements here:

Example: _I feel happiest when I am surrounded by people._

1. _____
2. _____
3. _____

4. _____

5. _____

6. _____

7. _____

8. _____

9. _____

10. _____

2 Develop Emotional Core Values

Beginning with a solid sense of your identity is essential for developing meaningful core values. Core values are the principles, standards, or qualities that you consider worthwhile or desirable. Personal values form the criterion for evaluating what is important in your life. Look at the words, phrases, and ideas you listed in your core value statements. Look for specific themes. Do any of the themes merge? Spend some time looking at the 10 statements and find the patterns within. Condense the 10 words, phrases, and ideas listed above into five core values that fit how you feel you should live your life. Utilize the values list from Chapter 3 to help in the creation of this list. Write the five emotional core values that you create here:

Example: *I want to be an empathetic listener and show love in ways others appreciate it the most.*

1. _____

2. _____

3. _____

4. _____

5. _____

3 Create Specific Personal Emotional Goals

Now it is time to create an action plan for your values! Creating effective personal goals fills the gap between who you are now and who you want to be. Review the core values that you have created and challenge yourself to develop specific actions (goals) for each one. What changes need to be made in your life to live by your core values? Remember, the best goals are S.M.A.R.T. (Specific, Measurable, Achievable, Realistic, and Timely). Begin by writing one personal goal for each core value here (you may wish to create more):

Example: *Seek out and befriend someone not like me within the next six months.*

1. _____

2. _____

3. _____

4. _____

5. _____

4 **Summarize Your Identity Area into an Emotional Identity Mission Statement**

Your identity, five core values, and personal goals are the building blocks for a successful identity area mission statement. Mission statements provide a synopsis of the strategy behind a set of individual goals; they are a short written description of your purpose and direction. Missions should be easy to remember and clarify where you want to go in life. In the personal space provided next, try to create a mission statement that summarizes your identity, values, and goals. Remember, mission statements are as unique as the individual creating them, and they don't need to be perfect!

Personal Space (My Emotional Mission)

_____
_____
_____
_____
_____
_____
_____
_____
_____
_____
_____
_____
_____
_____
_____
_____
_____

EMOTIONAL IDENTITY ALTERNATIVE ROUTES

The activities offered in this chapter should serve as an effective starting point for learning more about your emotional identity. The following sections provide numerous other resources and ideas that we would like to point you toward as you continue to explore who you are.

OBSERVE PEOPLE'S EMOTIONS

You can gain a great deal of perspective by observing and analyzing the ways in which others express their emotional identities. This can be as simple as "people watching," where you go to a populated area and simply observe the emotions that you see, how they impact others, and how the emotions interrelate. You can also ask others to observe your emotions and how you react to life.

For additional Web resources, try searching with the following terms:

Nonverbal communication

Rapport

Empathy

Watching emotions

ANALYZE YOUR DREAMS

Dream analysis is a positive way to understand your subconscious mind and how it can impact you in your conscious state. Emotions are rooted in the deepest parts of the mind, and many believe that dreams can give you insight about your emotional identity. Many psychotherapists can assist clients with dream analysis, and countless books on the topic are available.

For additional Web resources, try searching with the following terms:

Dream interpretation

Dream symbols

Subconscious

Meditation

START A JOURNAL

Journaling is a way to map your emotions over time, understand personal trends, and discover internal cycles. This book is an example of how journaling your responses to the included activities can reveal themes that you did not know existed. Finding a journal that fits your being is an important first step, so spend some time picking out the right one! Also, do not feel limited to just writing—journals often include sketches and other forms of expression.

For additional Web resources, try searching with the following terms:

Journaling

Diary

Personal expression

Memoir

The Physical
Identity Area

I AM CONVINCED THAT LIFE IN A PHYSICAL BODY IS MEANT TO BE

AN ECSTATIC EXPERIENCE.

■

—*SHATKI GAWAIN*

Your personal perspective of how you value your body.

The symbol used to signify physical identity is the rune *madr,* meaning "human," from the earliest Nordic rune alphabet. It is used here to symbolize the human body. Some researchers also indicate that it was an ancient pictorial representation of an athletic apparatus.

PHYSICAL IDENTITY

You have a unique physical being. The physical body that you possess is constantly being sent messages about how it compares to other bodies. You see these messages in fashion—men's shorts are getting longer, women's shorts are getting shorter. You see those messages in fitness—rippled muscles are the goal for men, being lean and toned is the goal for women. You see it in sports—records are being broken more frequently, and scandals involving performance-enhancing drugs are also more common. If you subscribe to society's rules, men should be muscled, fast, strong, tall, and have a full head of hair, straight white teeth, and a tan. Women apparently should be thin, toned, curvy in the "right" places, and not afraid to show some skin.

Health and medical science also give us "rules" for our bodies, and all with the goal of increasing quality and longevity of physical life. In the early 1900s, the average life expectancy was around 50 years and most deaths were caused by infections or acute diseases. Today, the average life expectancy is almost 80 years, thanks to antibiotics, immunizations, and advances in health care. Not surprisingly, the most common causes for death have changed. Now, 80 percent of all deaths in the United States are from chronic diseases resulting from lifestyles (Rosenstein, 1987). A sedentary lifestyle is now recognized as an actual health hazard (American College of Sports Medicine, 2000; Blair, 1993; Paffenbarger et al., 1993).

We are all born with differing abilities: strength, agility, flexibility, coordination, and so forth. We also all have disabilities that may come to us by way of genetics, training, illness, or accident. Abilities and disabilities are critical in understanding your physical identity. Regardless of your particular abilities and qualities, your physical identity is much more than that of a container; our bodies are the physical representation of our mind, spirit, and soul.

Many Americans struggle with their physical identity. Personal trainers are seeing an abundance of unrealistic health and fitness goals, with many people aspiring to transform their bodies into some airbrushed, computer-altered magazine model. It's no wonder so many people drop out of their exercise programs. A program with that kind of goal will probably never succeed, and the damage to personal motivation, self-image, and health is usually significant. Yet, you may continue to be inspired by rare and unrealistic ideals. Consider Lance Armstrong.

Lance Armstrong is perhaps one of the best known physical achievers in our recent history. With an unprecedented seven straight Tour de France wins, after a highly publicized battle with cancer, he is a symbol of physical perfection and perseverance. His story is the kind of "triumph over adversity" tale that people love.

So, if "triumph over adversity" is the recipe for a great physical accomplishment story, why don't we also see posters of the mother who safely gave birth to twins after bouncing back from numerous miscarriages? Why don't we stand in line for autographs from the premature baby who fights to survive and thrive when the doctors say it's impossible? How about the middle-aged father who makes the necessary changes to his nutrition and lifestyle and avoids a heart attack at age 45? Physical achievements come in many forms and are just one part of your physical identity.

We live in a culture that emphasizes appearance, and a particular kind of appearance that is often at odds with biology. As a result, many people develop a very negative image of their bodies and experience a great amount of shame if they do not conform to these cultural ideals. This negative body image can really decrease the quality of your life and sometimes leads to unhealthy eating/exercise behaviors. This book is a good place to start examining some of your assumptions about physical identity and to become more accepting and loving toward your body.

WE LIVE IN A CULTURE THAT EMPHASIZES APPEARANCE, AND A PARTICULAR KIND OF APPEARANCE THAT IS OFTEN AT ODDS WITH BIOLOGY.

SELF-TALK

Are you familiar with the concept of self-talk? Do you have an inner voice that speaks to you? This is a very simple concept but is very important in the process of getting a grip on your physical identity. Self-talk refers to the fact that you constantly have conversations with yourself in your head. There is nothing abnormal about this. It is as if you have an observer that monitors what you are doing and gives you feedback about your performance. Elite athletes know how to use self-talk to their advantage along with positive imagery. However, self-talk can be counterproductive when the content of it is primarily negative. This has a significant impact on your self-identity.

Similarly, you have private body talk—inner conversations that deal with your physical appearance. This private body talk profoundly influences how you feel about yourself. Where did you get your private body talk? From culture, family, friends, and so forth. You are in control of what you say to yourself.

Physical well-being means different things for different people. Some people have a self-defeating personal image of their bodies, some feel empowered and confident about their bodies, and for others physical self-concept is nothing more than the package that holds the person.

The body that you own has meaning to it well beyond the physical. You spend much of your life applying your level of comfort (or discomfort) with your body to many other areas of your life. For example, when Rob is upset about being overweight, it impacts his eating habits, he is more picky about what clothes he wears, he is less motivated to exercise, he is less comfortable in social situations so he avoids them, and he even begins to perceive food as a comfort. If you have discomfort with a part of your body, you may choose to cover it, augment it, or commit large amounts of money to fix it. If you have blemishes, you cover them, color them, or seek out medications to eradicate them. This may not apply to everyone, but it certainly captures the actions of a large part of our American society.

THE BODY THAT YOU OWN HAS MEANING TO IT WELL BEYOND THE PHYSICAL.

The human body is basically the wrapper for your soul. Your body is naturally occurring, and your being cannot be contained by your physical body alone. Paradoxically, your body holds a physical history of who you are. Many believe you can even give impressions of where your life is going by studying your body. Biological predictors and heredity, along with beliefs such as aura reading and palmistry, give credence to the idea that your body represents more than soft tissue, organs, and bones.

You will need to understand the impact that your physical self-image has on your overall life to create your physical core values and mission statement. Do you have a love–hate relationship with your body? Do you spend great amounts of your energy hiding, covering, or obsessing over a part of your physical being that you dislike? Or is physical identity an area of confidence for you, a stable, comfortable, and strong aspect of your life? Or does your physical identity give you false confidence because you are perceived as being closer to "the ideal"?

As you develop your physical identity, you will combat some of the challenging messages that you hold over your body. You will also have opportunity to celebrate your unique physical being. As you learn more about how you interact with the physical world, keep in mind that the negative emotions that you may feel probably are not born from within you. These bodily self-perceptions are a product of a society obsessed with unrealistic expectations.

> " Our own physical body possesses a wisdom which we who inhabit the body lack."
>
> —HENRY MILLER

PHYSICAL IDENTITY FOCUS POINTS AND ACTIVITIES

Your physical identity is rooted in your personal perspective of how you relate to your physical being. It is the cumulative effect of your physical attributes, how you feel about your body, and even the messages that others feed you about your body.

As you complete the activities in this chapter, which are summarized in the following list, remember to keep track of reoccurring themes that present themselves to you. What types of values are you seeing repeatedly? How do your discoveries in these activities help you to better understand yourself? What topics reappear as areas that are intriguing? What are you learning about how you learn and how you best take in and store information?

Activity 1: Physical Identity Physical (PIP). This activity asks you to "inventory" your perception of your physical habits and behaviors. It is not judged or compared to any kind of "standard." Instead, it will be up to you to review your PIP and determine what it means for yourself. The important piece to this activity is exploring your reactions and self-judgments.

Activity 2: Anatomy 101. In this activity, you will get more specific about what you think of your body. You will actually draw a rough portrait of your body (just symbolic; this is not an art contest). Then you will label and describe significant parts of your body portrait that are most important to you. The value of this activity is explaining why you represented the labels the way you did. For example, if you emphasized your ears in your drawing, was it because you think you have big ears or because you think you hear well?

Activity 3: Media Watchdog. In this exercise, you will spend some time with a TV and a magazine or two doing a quick count of "ideal" physical images versus "realistic" physical images. You can probably predict what will happen, but actually going through the activity can be a real eye opener! Use this experience to explore what impact the media is having on your physical identity.

Activity 4: Reflective Relationships. How do you physically perceive the people you hang out with? Are your friends a picture of what you want to be? Do you associate with people who are physically "worse" than you in order to feel better about yourself? Maybe you haven't really thought about this before, and you associate with people regardless of your perception of them physically. Nonetheless, try it out, and see what you can learn about yourself through this meaningful reflection.

activity 1 PHYSICAL IDENTITY PHYSICAL (PIP)

Going to the doctor's office for a physical exam is an important step in monitoring your health. The information gathered helps the doctor to decide what is needed for your improved health by determining what things are problematic and what things are doing well. Anxieties aside, a visit to a physician gives you a baseline reading of your personal physical condition, as well as some instructions that you need to follow (exercise more, eat less sweets, etc.).

This activity will ask you to serve as your own doctor and create your own prognosis regarding the current condition of your physical identity. One major challenge is that a physician is objective and you are not. As you fill out the PIP form, it will be difficult at times to be honest with yourself. This is an important part of this activity, because the areas that you have trouble completing are likely areas that need the most focus.

THE STEP BY STEP

1 Begin by completing the PIP form (Figure 7–1). Please fill out every section even if you have to skip one at first and return to it later. You may need to access medical records for some of the PIP, and you will need to measure parts of yourself (weight, height, etc.).

2 Now that you have completed the PIP, go back and look at what you have written about yourself. If you find areas where you would like to change, proceed to the PIP Change Worksheet (Figure 7–2) and begin by writing about why that area is difficult for you. It is important that you isolate why this area is so challenging.

3 Next, also on the PIP Change Worksheet (Figure 7–2), write a prescription for an ideal or improved physical identity in each of these areas. How do you define "ideal physical shape" or "ideal health"? Picture yourself that way. Compare that to your notes in Figure 7–1 and take notice of where there are differences. Based on your examination, what prescriptions would you write for yourself? Write them down.

4 Finally, describe how you know when you have reached your goal. What would a more successful physical identity look and feel like to you?

" ————————
I told the doctor I broke my leg in two places. He told me to quit going to those places."

—HENNY YOUNGMAN

Physical Identity Physical (PIP) Form

Name: _____   Age: _____   Sex: _____

Height: _____   Weight: _____   Occupation : _____

Please list all of your current health issues/challenges.

_____

_____

Please list any medications (current and past) and any nutritional supplements/herbs that you are taking.

_____

_____

Have you ever been hospitalized or injured? Please list each occasion.

_____

_____

Did you have any childhood illnesses? Please list any that you had and how long they impacted your physical identity.

_____

_____

What is the history of your family's health (parents and siblings)? Are there any health issues that you need to be aware of as you move through life?

_____

_____

How many hours of sleep do you regularly get per day? How would you rate the quality of your sleep; that is, do you wake up frequently, have a hard time falling asleep, etc.? If yes, what do you think may be the cause of your challenged sleep? Write down your detailed sleep habits.

_____

_____

How would you rate your eating habits? Do you eat five to seven servings of fruits and vegetables daily? Do you tend to eat fast food, foods high in sugar and fat, or foods that are mass produced and contain very little nutritional value? Write down a thorough list of foods you typically eat and how frequently you eat them.

_____

_____

FIGURE 7–1 Physical Identity Physical Form

Do you drink alcohol, smoke cigarettes, or take any other types of drugs such as prescriptions, steroids, psychotropic drugs, pain killers, etc.? Write down how much you use any of these substances and how often you use them in detail.

_____

_____

What kinds of exercise do you regularly engage in? Do you do cardiovascular exercise three times per week for 20 minutes? Do you have habits and/or a lifestyle that allows you to naturally find time for exercise? Write down your current exercise habits, including cardio and noncardio.

_____

_____

How would you rate your stress level? Do you often feel like you are at your "wit's end"? How much of your day is spent feeling frantic?

_____

_____

Do you relax? Do you have time to be calm, meditate, and slow things down a bit? What types of things do you do to relax? Write down your relaxation habits.

_____

_____

Are you sexually active? If so, are your personal needs for sexual release substantially met? Write about your personal sexual satisfaction level and how that impacts your physical identity.

_____

_____

How do you relate to your own body? Are you happy with your physical makeup? What parts of you are you most pleased with, and what parts would you change if you could?

_____

_____

Are there any other items that you feel need to be mentioned that have not been addressed through the previous questions? Please write them here.

_____

_____

FIGURE 7–1 *continued*

Physical Identity Physical Change Worksheet

AREA OF NEEDED CHANGE #1: _____

What are the things that make this change area challenging?

_____

_____

Your prescription for a better physical identity:

_____

_____

How will you know when you have succeeded?

_____

_____

AREA OF NEEDED CHANGE #2: _____

What are the things that make this change area challenging?

_____

_____

Your prescription for a better physical identity:

_____

_____

How will you know when you have succeeded?

_____

_____

AREA OF NEEDED CHANGE #3: _____

What are the things that make this change area challenging?

_____

_____

Your prescription for a better physical identity:

_____

_____

FIGURE 7–2 PIP Change Worksheet

How will you know when you have succeeded?

_____

_____

AREA OF NEEDED CHANGE #4: _____

What are the things that make this change area challenging?

_____

_____

Your prescription for a better physical identity:

_____

_____

How will you know when you have succeeded?

_____

_____

AREA OF NEEDED CHANGE #5: _____

What are the things that make this change area challenging?

_____

_____

Your prescription for a better physical identity:

_____

_____

How will you know when you have succeeded?

_____

_____

FIGURE 7–2 *continued*

Reflections

The task of filling out the PIP creates a thorough medical and health history for you to consider. As you no doubt have guessed, the take-home message for this activity is not your history per se. It is more about what that history means when you think of your physical identity. The prescriptions that you wrote for yourself will be a vital tool for understanding what you feel is a priority in your physical identity.

What parts of the PIP held the greatest meaning for you? On which did you find yourself pausing and spending great amounts of time?

When you wrote your personal prescriptions, did you notice any reoccurring themes? Did you focus on any particular areas of your physical being or health?

Review the writing that you did regarding what success would look like physically. What ideas do you have that might help you gain clarity about your physical identity and health goals?

Personal Space

This is your opportunity to add your own thoughts and make notes.

_____

_____

_____

_____

_____

_____

_____

_____

_____

_____

_____

_____

_____

_____

_____

_____

activity 2 **ANATOMY 101**

Anatomy is the study of the physical body. In this activity, you will address the idea of anatomy from a personal perspective and will be asked to self-assess the parts of you with which you are most comfortable, and those areas with which you are less comfortable. By creating a self-portrait of your body, you will gain insight into some of your physical core values.

If you are like many people, the idea of analyzing your personal anatomy is approached with some trepidation. Many people are taught to be ashamed of their bodies for a variety of reasons. This belief may make this one of the more difficult activities in the workbook. Do your best. By overcoming these negative messages, you will truly begin to know your potential physical identity.

THE STEP BY STEP

 Draw a picture of yourself in the space provided on the following page. Be as detailed as you can, symbolizing your physical body the way you perceive it. Be complete and be thorough; this drawing will be important when considering your physical identity.

 Do not feel limited by any rules. You can add other objects, people, animals, aids, ideas, or symbols that you would like. Try to capture in this drawing whatever helps symbolize how you see yourself physically.

 After you have completed your drawing, label and describe the parts of you that have significance. Use the following as a guide:

- The parts of your body with which you are most/least comfortable.

- The parts of your body you can/cannot change.

- The articles of clothing that you drew.

- The parts of your body that you drew in particular detail.

- The parts of your body that you drew that are larger or smaller in comparison to the rest of your body.

- All other objects, people, ideas, or symbols that you added to your portrait.

- Add any other labels you want to that we have not listed.

 Now that your picture is complete, take a moment to evaluate in Figure 7–3 how satisfied (or dissatisfied) you are with different areas of your body. If there is a feature of your body you want to rate that is not listed, just write it in and rate your level of satisfaction.

How satisfied are you with each area of your body?

1. Very Dissatisfied

2. Mostly Dissatisfied

3. Neither Satisfied nor Dissatisfied

ACTIVITY PURPOSE

To create a self-portrait of yourself that effectively demonstrates your relationship with your physical identity. ◼

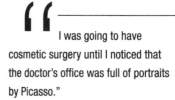

I was going to have cosmetic surgery until I noticed that the doctor's office was full of portraits by Picasso."

—*RITA RUDNER*

4. Mostly Satisfied

5. Very Satisfied

Add your ratings and make sure your score is between 10 and 50. Find your range in the grid shown in Figure 7–4, and see if the generalized description helps you begin to understand your physical identity better. If not, make some notes about why that description does not fit you and how it should indicate the way you feel about yourself. What parts of that description do you identify with? Which parts do not connect?

SELF-RATINGS

Face (facial features, complexion, etc.) _____

Hair (color, thickness, texture, etc.) _____

Lower torso (buttocks, hips, thighs, legs, etc.) _____

Midtorso (waist, stomach, etc.) _____

Upper torso (chest or breasts, shoulders, arms, etc.) _____

Muscle tone _____

Weight _____

Height _____

Skin (tone, marks, hair, etc.) _____

Movement (coordination, grace, etc.) _____

FIGURE 7–3 Physical Self-Ratings

SCORE RANGE	DESCRIPTION
10–19	I am significantly unhappy with many areas of my body. In fact, there are very few things about my body that I like. It sometimes keeps me from going out with friends or participating in physical activities, and I often wear clothes that attempt to hide my body. I frequently complain about my body (to others, and to myself) and have become so discouraged about it that I have been depressed sometimes. I have even considered "extreme" diets/makeovers/exercise programs or surgery.
20–29	I have the body I have and I can't do anything about it. There are lots of things I don't like about my body, but I try not to let it consume my life. I try to keep my body healthy, and I always say that's more important to me than appearance. However, I sometimes secretly wish that I could achieve a certain look, and occasionally I get really motivated to make some changes.
30–39	I am comfortable in my body, and I enjoy the body I have. I recognize that there are more attractive bodies than mine, but there are also lots of bodies that aren't as attractive as mine. I'm thankful for the body I have, and I am pretty good about keeping it that way. There are times that I'm even very good about treating my body well, and I take it seriously. Others have complimented me on my body or appearance, and it makes me feel a little uncomfortable, but inside I like hearing it.
40–50	I am very happy with the body I have. I am comfortable participating in physical activities or wearing clothing that reveals my body/shape. I enjoy the attention and compliments I receive for my appearance and have done things to attract such attention. Sometimes I even admire my own body in the mirror. Inside, I secretly fear negative changes to my body, and I do things to avoid harming my appearance.

FIGURE 7–4 Self-Score Descriptions

Reflections

Evaluating your own anatomy can be pretty difficult. We are sent frequent messages about our bodies from others; thus we all carry baggage and oftentimes a perverted sense of self.

Why are you comfortable/uncomfortable with particular parts of your body?

What parts of your body are you the most/least comfortable with and why?

What parts of your body do you feel you can change/cannot change and why?

If you drew articles of clothing on your illustration, why did you draw them?

What parts of your body did you draw in detail, and why?

What parts of your body did you draw particularly large/small in comparison to others?

What objects, people, ideas, or symbols did you add to the picture and why?

What labels did you add and why?

What is your reaction to your self-rating of your body?

Personal Space

_____

_____

_____

_____

_____

_____

_____

_____

_____

_____

_____

_____

_____

_____

_____

activity 3   MEDIA WATCHDOG

The influence of media is so omnipresent that we do not often notice it. This exercise will challenge you to use your critical eye on the media. Specifically, you will spend some time watching TV and looking through a magazine. Throughout this activity, you will be counting, documenting, and recording what you see. It is one thing to read in a book or hear someone tell you that the media is impacting our physical identity, but it is another thing totally to see it for yourself!

THE STEP BY STEP

Carve out 60 minutes to watch prime time TV on a major TV network. It doesn't have to be all at once or even on the same day. However, you are going to watch TV differently than you might usually watch it. You are going to turn off the sound and take notes for 10-minute segments. It might be helpful to use a timer that you can set to 10-minute intervals. Specifically, you will use the Television Watchdog Log (Figure 7–5) to document the number of times you notice each of the listed items. Some of them are obvious, some may show up more subtly, but you will likely have no trouble spotting them if you are paying attention and looking for them.

Afterward, try the same process with a fashion magazine, or another popular magazine, using chunks of five pages instead of minutes and recording your observations on Figure 7–6. Go page by page and see what you find when looking with this "watchdog" lens. You do not have to read everything. You should be primarily scanning for images, titles, and headline words that catch your attention. Be sure to include advertisements as well.

> No matter how much spin, effort, lunch, or dinner you give the media, they will not fail to notice whether you have won or lost."
>
> —*ROBIN RENWICK*

Television Watchdog Log

For the first 10 minutes of observation, count the number of . . .

Overweight people . . .

_____

Fit people . . .

_____

Sexy people . . .

_____

Ugly people . . .

_____

During your second 10 minutes of observation, count the number of . . .

People with straight, white teeth . . .

_____

People with crooked, damaged, or discolored teeth . . .

_____

People with strong confident smiles . . .

_____

People with hesitant, nervous smiles . . .

_____

During your third 10 minutes of observation, count the number of . . .

Men with visible, "ripped" muscles . . .

_____

Men who are less muscular or "skinny" . . .

_____

Women whose body parts are stereotypically attractive . . .

_____

Women who have less "attractive" bodies . . .

_____

During your fourth 10 minutes of observation, count the number of . . .

People with attractive complexions, clear skin, or heavily covered with makeup . . .

_____

People with unattractive complexions, who have blemishes, or are "natural" . . .

_____

During your fifth 10 minutes of observation, count the number of . . .

People who are actively exercising, playing a sport, or working out . . .

_____

People who are sedentary . . .

_____

During your last 10 minutes of observation, count the number of . . .

People eating healthful foods . . .

_____

People eating junk foods . . .

_____

FIGURE 7–5
Television Watchdog Log

Magazine Watchdog Log

For the first five pages of observation, count the number of . . .

Overweight people . . .

_____

Fit people . . .

_____

Sexy people . . .

_____

Ugly people . . .

_____

During your second five pages of observation, count the number of . . .

People with straight, white teeth . . .

_____

People with crooked, damaged, or discolored teeth . . .

_____

People with strong confident smiles . . .

_____

People with hesitant, nervous smiles . . .

_____

During your third five pages of observation, count the number of . . .

Men with visible, "ripped" muscles . . .

_____

Men who are less muscular or "skinny" . . .

_____

Women whose body parts are stereotypically attractive . . .

_____

Women who have less "attractive" bodies . . .

_____

During your fourth five pages of observation, count the number of . . .

People with attractive complexions, clear skin, or heavily covered with makeup . . .

_____

People with unattractive complexions, who have blemishes, or are "natural" . . .

_____

During your fifth five pages of observation, count the number of . . .

People who are actively exercising, playing a sport, or working out . . .

_____

People who are sedentary . . .

_____

During your last five pages of observation, count the number of . . .

People eating healthful foods . . .

_____

People eating junk foods . . .

_____

FIGURE 7–6
Magazine Watchdog Log

Reflections

In logging the images that you saw while being a watchdog, you probably began to notice the level at which the mass media sends us messages about how we should look. The ideal person as imagined by our media is nearly impossible to create in real life, but you probably find yourself trying from time to time. We forget that people get posed, airbrushed, and of course often get more than one "take" to get things right. Life is just not like that.

Was this activity difficult or easy?

What surprised you? Why do you think it surprised you?

What did your brief media scan tell you about the messages we get regarding our physical identity?

What impact do those messages have on you? Do any of them make you angry, inspired, motivated, happy, or confused? Why do you think they have that ability to affect you?

Now, think about the fact that you looked for these things in short 10-minute intervals. What do you think you'd see if your intervals were a full hour long?

So what does all this tell you about your physical identity? How much influence does the media have on your physical identity?

Personal Space

_____

_____

_____

_____

_____

_____

_____

_____

_____

_____

_____

_____

_____

_____

activity 4 REFLECTIVE RELATIONSHIPS

Many studies on social dynamics suggest that we choose our relationships for meaningful reasons. Some theorists think we tend to spend time with people who make us feel better about ourselves. Others think that we gravitate toward the people we wish to be like. In considering your physical identity, you can see how this can become quite important. If you are choosing to be around people who are physically like you, and you find yourself rejecting people who are different, you are limiting yourself. Your selectiveness of peers based on your physical identity also impacts who you seek out for sexual partnerships.

THE STEP BY STEP

1 In Figure 7–7, list the five people to whom you are the closest, spend the most time with, and feel the most like.

2 Indicate how you compare to each person physically, in your own perception. Are they in shape (or out of shape) like you? Are they physically attractive? Do they maintain a level of sexual attraction (not necessarily always to you, but in general)? Physically, what is it about this person that makes him or her similar to you?

3 Now, how is each person different? What unique characteristics do they possess that make them quite different than you? What are the definite distinctions between your five peers and you that make you unique?

Reflections

It probably felt a bit odd to think of your friends in terms of their physical identities. This activity asks you to consider with whom you choose to relate physically. Give some thought to the similarities that you have with your peers, how that can be a benefit, and how it can be a real liability.

What were some of the consistent traits that you share with your five peers? Why do you think you all share these qualities? What is it about your physical identities that brings you together?

What variety could you find in your peer group? Do you find that you are closest with people who represent varying levels of attractiveness? Or do you find that you are really narrow in your friend selection?

What personal insecurities about your body impact your relationship choices? For example, if you are very thin, do you tend to avoid larger people? If you consider yourself very attractive, do you tend to avoid people who seem less attractive than you?

Do you find that you avoid contact with people who have a disability or who have obvious physical differences? Is anyone on your list differently abled?

How can you open up your physical identity so that you can relate to people who are very different than you physically?

" Sexually, we are all competing for the same seat on the bus and the thing that holds it together is the tightly held conceit that we are all sexual gods. How can I believe in my own uniqueness when there's a cat out there exactly the same as me?"

—*JEFF MELVIN, FROM THE TELEVISION PROGRAM* NORTHERN EXPOSURE

Physical Relationship Reflections

NAME OF PERSON #1: _____

How is this person similar to you with regard to his or her physical identity?

_____

_____

How is this person different than you with regard to his or her physical identity?

_____

_____

NAME OF PERSON #2: _____

How is this person similar to you with regard to his or her physical identity?

_____

_____

How is this person different than you with regard to his or her physical identity?

_____

_____

NAME OF PERSON #3: _____

How is this person similar to you with regard to his or her physical identity?

_____

_____

How is this person different than you with regard to his or her physical identity?

_____

_____

NAME OF PERSON #4: _____

How is this person similar to you with regard to his or her physical identity?

_____

_____

How is this person different than you with regard to his or her physical identity?

_____

_____

NAME OF PERSON #5: _____

How is this person similar to you with regard to his or her physical identity?

_____

_____

How is this person different than you with regard to his or her physical identity?

_____

_____

FIGURE 7–7

Physical Relationship Reflections

Personal Space

_____

_____

_____

_____

_____

_____

_____

_____

_____

_____

_____

_____

_____

_____

_____

PHYSICAL IDENTITY PERSONAL VISION PYRAMID

It is time now to make meaning out of the activities you have just completed. Using the Vision Pyramid, you will channel the energy within you to learn about your true identity.

 What Is My Physical Identity?

As you progressed through the activities in this chapter, you no doubt began to notice consistent themes and ideas. Look through these activities and find 10 words, phrases, and ideas that are regularly occurring themes throughout your activity notes. Translate these themes into short statements to describe your physical identity. It is important to avoid making judgments at this point; they apply to core values in the following step. Simply pull out the observed themes. Write these 10 themes/statements here:

Example: _I recognize that physical fitness is vital to feeling good about myself, and that I need to be consistent with fitness._

1. _____

2. _____

3. _____

4. _____

5. _____

6. _____

7. _____

8. _____

9. _____

10. _____

2 Develop Physical Core Values

Beginning with a solid sense of your identity is essential for developing meaningful core values. Core values are the principles, standards, or qualities that you consider worthwhile or desirable. Personal values form the criterion for evaluating what is important in your life. Look at the words, phrases, and ideas you listed in your core value statements. Look for specific themes. Do any of the themes merge? Spend some time looking at the 10 statements and find the patterns within. Condense the 10 words, phrases, and ideas listed above into five core values that fit how you feel you should live your life. Utilize the values list from Chapter 3 to help in the creation of this list. Write the five physical core values that you create here:

Example: *cardiovascular fitness, feeling healthy and vibrant*

1. _____

2. _____

3. _____

4. _____

5. _____

3 Create Specific Personal Physical Goals

Now it is time to create an action plan for your values! Creating effective personal goals fills the gap between who you are now and who you want to be. Review the core values that you have created and challenge yourself to develop specific actions (goals) for each one. What changes need to be made in your life to live by your core values? Remember, the best goals are S.M.A.R.T. (Specific, Measurable, Achievable, Realistic, and Timely). Begin by writing one personal goal for each core value here (you may wish to create more):

Example: *I will continue to ride my bike roughly 50 miles per week throughout the summer months.*

1. _____

2. _____

3. _____

4. _____

5. _____

4 **Summarize Your Identity Area into a Physical Identity Mission Statement**

Your identity, five core values, and personal goals are the building blocks for a successful identity area mission statement. Mission statements provide a synopsis of the strategy behind a set of individual goals; they are a short written description of your purpose and direction. Missions should be easy to remember and clarify where you want to go in life. In the personal space provided next, try to create a mission statement that summarizes your identity, values, and goals. Remember, mission statements are as unique as the individual creating them, and they don't need to be perfect!

Personal Space (My Physical Mission)

_____

_____

_____

_____

_____

_____

_____

_____

_____

_____

_____

_____

_____

_____

_____

PHYSICAL IDENTITY ALTERNATIVE ROUTES

The activities offered in this chapter should serve as an effective starting point for learning more about your physical identity. The following sections provide numerous other resources and ideas that we would like to point you toward as you continue to explore who you are.

LEARN ABOUT NUTRITION

A great deal of information is available on the subject of nutrition. The concern over fad diets and the negative impact that they can have may very well motivate you to seek out real nutrition information. Nutritionists are a great place to start. They can analyze your personal habits and suggest tips for healthier living. Your personal physician or medical provider is another great source. Finally, look in your community for workshops and courses that can give you in-depth information about nutrition. One tip: Avoid nutritional advice that is not backed by a professional.

For additional Web resources, try searching with the following terms:

Nutrition

Food pyramid

USDA

Organic food

CREATE A PERSONAL EXERCISE PLAN

There are countless resources for you to discover if you want to get into shape! Personal trainers have specific knowledge to help you understand your body and what you need to create a safe and healthy plan. Even your local community health club may have staff that can assist you with creating a good plan. Your medical provider is another excellent and usually free resource (exercise = better health!).

For additional Web resources, try searching with the following terms:

Fitness

Exercise plan

Physical trainer

Safe exercise

UNDERSTAND HOLISTIC HEALTH PERSPECTIVES

Western medicine is quickly embracing traditional remedies and practices from around the world, such as acupuncture, the power of massage, and even natural, nondrug remedies. There are numerous holistic health providers, and it is important to make sure that you study the credentials of the person you choose to see. Numerous books and magazines also focus on these quickly growing health techniques.

**For additional Web resources,
try searching with the following terms:**

Holistic health

Eastern medicine

Mind body

Alternative medicine

REFERENCES

American College of Sports Medicine (2000). *ACSM's guidelines for exercise testing and prescription* (6th ed.). Philadelphia: Lippincott Williams & Wilkins.

Blair, S. N. (1993). 1993 C. H. McCloy research lecture: Physical activity, physical fitness, and health. *Research Quarterly for Exercise and Sport, 64*(4), 365–378.

Paffenbarger, R. S., et al. (1993). The association of changes in physical activity level and other lifestyle characteristics with mortality among men. *New England Journal of Medicine, 328*, 538–545.

Rosenstein, A. (1987). The benefits of health maintenance. *The Physician and Sportsmedicine, 15*, 57–69.

The Spiritual Identity Area

CHAPTER

Your personal perspective of your religious, ethical, and/or sacred beliefs.

The symbol used to signify spiritual identity comes from a symbol used by early Native Americans to indicate soul, essence, and spirit. Researchers believe the half-circle in the middle represented the sunrise, and the line below represented the horizon. The earth was an honored and powerful spirit in many Native American cultures.

A DIVINE LIFE FORCE PERMEATES EVERY INCH OF THE UNIVERSE.

SPIRIT ANIMATES MATTER AND INSPIRES THE DREAMS OF HUMANITY.

■

—*BRIAN LUKE SEAWARD*

SPIRITUAL IDENTITY

Spirituality stems from what you determine is right or wrong, the meaning of life, your origin, your purpose, and your source of spiritual energy. This chapter will look at your spiritual identity from many perspectives, with the purpose of exploration—not indoctrination. You should feel comfortable exploring your spirituality without pressure to conform to any specific set of beliefs.

THIS CHAPTER WILL LOOK AT YOUR SPIRITUAL IDENTITY FROM MANY

PERSPECTIVES, WITH THE PURPOSE OF EXPLORATION—NOT INDOCTRINATION.

Beliefs built on your ethics create guiding principles for what your purpose, meaning, and place is in the world and beyond. Your beliefs may stem from an established religion or may be unique to you. Regardless of faith, your spiritual identity is rooted in the animating force or source of vitality, energy, and strength that inspires you to be you. For some, this is through ceremony and ritualistic faith; for others, it may be a literal stroll in the woods.

Understanding of your spiritual identity begins with exploring the ethical standards that you apply to yourself and others. These standards are important factors in determining how you behave and feel. Oftentimes your ethics are built on a set of beliefs based on religion, social upbringing, a gut feeling, or past experience. Regardless of the source of these beliefs, they are critical in determining what motivates you and what doesn't. Harnessing this motivation allows you to work toward doing what you feel is right and good. It propels you into action on matters that are most important to you.

SPIRITUALITY FROM FOUR PERSPECTIVES

Spirituality can be viewed from four thematic areas: ethics, core beliefs, religion, and spirit (Figure 8–1). Each perspective is as important and valid as the other. You may find your spirituality drawing from one or from all of these four areas. This idea of spirituality may broaden your preconceived notions of spirituality; indeed, many people do not think of themselves as spiritual beings. You are.

ETHICS

ETHICS

Your personal doctrine of what is right, just, and good when relating to others.

" Ethics is not definable, is not implementable, because it is not conscious; it involves not only our thinking, but also our feeling."

—VALDEMAR W. SETZER

Ethics help you to determine what is right and wrong and give you guidance in knowing how to act in complicated situations. They can be a bit gray for you. In some situations you know exactly what your ethics are; at other times you question them. Your ethics stem from teachings from a parent, religion, friend, or they may just simply "feel" right. Regardless of the source of these ethical values, the practice of applying these ethics is critical to your identity.

Your ethics are as unique as the patterns on your fingerprints. Ethics come from individual experiences, from teachings by parents, friends, spiritual leaders, and the media. Some ethical beliefs you may feel are simply intrinsic to you. This is what makes your spirituality unique. Because of that individualization, your spirituality is often tested the most when in opposition to other people's beliefs. For example, if you believe that honesty is a key ethical value and you witness a close friend tell a lie, you will need to decide what action to take. Ethics focus primarily on your relationship with others. How should you treat others? How should others treat you?

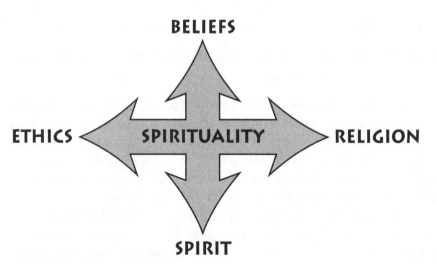

FIGURE 8–1 The Four Thematic Areas of Spirituality

CORE BELIEFS

Beliefs are assertions of truth and are formed by the ethical framework unique to you. Some truths form guiding principles that shape what your perceptions are of your origin, purpose, meaning, and place in the world. These core beliefs act as a rudder steering you in one direction or another. They shape how you behave, treat others, relate with nature, and think of yourself. Changing your core beliefs can result in significant changes to your identity. For this reason many people turn to religion. However, core beliefs can also change as a result of study, critical events, or close relationships with others.

On a very simple level, everyone has beliefs. They are critical to our conscious minds. They serve the purpose of explaining those matters that you cannot see, hear, touch, or feel immediately. It is important for you to investigate all of your beliefs because they shape how you perceive reality. You may be missing out on some great things by not challenging your own perceptions.

CORE BELIEFS are guiding principles for your origin, purpose, meaning, and place in the world.

RELIGION

Religion plays a critical role in many people's lives. A resurgence of traditional religious practice is being seen on a worldwide scale. One group (www.adherents.com) has predicted that one of the 10 great trends of the twenty-first century will be a movement toward greater religiosity. There are literally thousands of recognized religions in the world, some with billions of believers, and others with but a handful.

In the most rudimentary of senses, religion establishes a shared set of truths that provide order, reason, and purpose to a world filled with mysteries. As Ralph Waldo Emerson once said, "Every natural fact is a symbol of some spiritual fact." Without spiritual beliefs, you are left questioning "why" to nearly everything. For example: Why is there gravity, what created gravity, did gravity's creator create me? Where do you find answers to these questions? Some turn internally, others to science, but many turn to spiritual leaders in the form of religion. It is these religious beliefs that explain the unknown and provide comfort and commonality for large groups of people.

RELIGION is a set of beliefs, values, and practices based on the teachings of a spiritual leader.

SPIRIT

The fourth and final perception of spirituality is focused on your "spirit." Everyone is born with a spirit. It is the animating force or source of vitality, energy, strength, and inner peace in your life. Some may call it the spark of life, some call it soul, and others simply refer to it as the energy within us. Spirit is literally the electric charge that runs through our neurons. This spark fluctuates in intensity over most of your life, propelling you to action and hopefully bringing you closer to a sense of inner peace. Your body and emotions act as pathways channeling this energy to motivate your every move and thought.

A spirit is a deeply personal thing. Every spirit is different. You may find that music lifts your spirit, or art, adventure, nature, friendships, and so forth. Whatever it is that creates harmony within you is worth seeking out and holding on to. By focusing on your spirit, you can intensify this spark, which will result in more energy, peace, and vitality.

SPIRIT is the animating force or source of vitality, energy, strength, and inner peace.

> " Faith may be defined briefly as an illogical belief in the occurrence of the improbable."
>
> —H. L. MENCKEN

> " My religion consists of a humble admiration of the illimitable superior spirit who reveals himself in the slight details we are able to perceive with our frail and feeble mind."
>
> —ALBERT EINSTEIN

> " Every time you don't follow your inner guidance, you feel a loss of energy, loss of power, a sense of spiritual deadness."
>
> —SHATKI GAWAIN

You also have the ability to magnify your spirit yourself by focusing internally and doing things that bring you happiness, confidence, and joy. Think about a time when your spirit burned the brightest. These are the moments that bring out your best.

The four areas of spirituality (ethics, core beliefs, religion, and spirit) can be measured by an old adage. This adage asks the simple question: "How full is your pitcher?" Imagine your spiritual self as a pitcher that can be filled with your beliefs, core ethics, religion, and spirit. When your pitcher is full, you are at peace, things are in balance, and life seems to be "working." When your pitcher is empty, you feel a void, an absence, or a nagging feeling, as if you are missing something. It is hoped that the activities in this chapter will give you a greater sense of how to fill your pitcher with the good stuff!

SPIRITUAL IDENTITY FOCAL POINTS AND ACTIVITIES

Your spiritual identity is rooted in how your ethics, core beliefs, religion, and spirit come together to guide you.

As you complete the activities in this chapter, which are summarized in the following list, remember to keep track of reoccurring themes that present themselves to you. What types of values are you seeing repeatedly? How do your discoveries in these activities help you to better understand yourself? What topics reappear as areas that are intriguing? What are you learning about how you learn and how you best take in and store information?

Activity 1: Ethics in Action. This activity is designed to help you root out the source of what is right, just, and good in a difficult situation. The activity begins with a hypothetical ethical dilemma. You are tasked with developing questions to determine your personal ethical response. Along the way you will prioritize issues and determine importance.

Activity 2: Spiritual Lifelines. This activity is designed to organize the important ethical/spiritual events that have occurred in your life, establishing a personal history of spirituality. You will respond to a number of questions that will help to jog your memory about key events in your life. These events helped establish your spiritual belief system.

Activity 3: Ethical/Spiritual/Religious Role Models. This activity will explore the important ethical, spiritual, or religious role models in your life. These individuals play an important role in shaping your beliefs. They help to clarify direction in your ethical/spiritual/religious life by setting a good example for you to follow. You will examine these individuals and personalize the lessons that they shared to make meaning of your unique spiritual identity.

Activity 4: What Is Good in Your Life. You will make an extensive list of what is good in your life in this activity. The best way to feel good is to think good. Whether you call it counting your blessings, bringing about good karma, or simply paying attention to good things, the result is the same: positive spiritual energy.

Activity 5: Spiritual Coat of Arms. A coat of arms is a symbol of family honor and values. You will create your own spiritual coat of arms to represent what is most important to you spiritually. This activity will challenge you to think deeply about your spiritual and religious beliefs.

To help you root out the source of what is right, just, and good in a difficult situation. ◼

" Action indeed is the sole medium of expression for ethics."

—*JANE ADDAMS*

activity 1 ETHICS IN ACTION

It is time to test your ethics. Included below is a short ethical scenario designed to help you determine what right, just, and good in a difficult situation. Take your time on this activity. Be sure to ask the question "why" enough times to root out the source of your ethics.

THE STEP BY STEP

1 Read over the following scenario. Take a moment to think of what you would do if you were actually faced with this situation. What questions would come to mind? What kind of system would you create to prioritize your ethics and beliefs?

> *Scenario:* Imagine you are a doctor working with four people who are struggling to survive a deadly illness. The illness moves quickly and there is not enough time to seek out advice and counsel of other doctors. You only have enough antidote to save one of the four people. Time is too short to explore other options. Act now or all four will die immediately. One of the four people is a loved one. The second person is a beloved mentor, the third person is a colleague, and the fourth person is a complete stranger.

2 Formulate the five most important ethical questions you need to ask in order to determine what to do next. (For example: Which of the relationships with the four people do I value the most?).

1. _____
2. _____
3. _____
4. _____
5. _____

3 To put your ethical framework and beliefs to the test, you now need to answer your own questions. Since this activity is a hypothetical situation, you are free to make up your own answers. You need to recognize and accept the difficulty in doing this. In the following spaces, answer your own questions.

1. _____
2. _____
3. _____
4. _____
5. _____

 Now that you have created some tough questions and answered them, it is time to complete the task at hand.

Determine the order of whom you would save with the anti-
dote and give an explanation for each person:

1. _____
2. _____
3. _____
4. _____
5. _____

Reflections

Now that your ethics have been tested and you investigated the roots of your
ethical principles, consider the following questions. In the future, when ethical
situations are presented to you, use this process to gain clarity.

Which of the five questions that you created was the most difficult to
answer? Which of the five was the easiest? Why?

When have you applied the ethical principles that you used to complete
this activity in your daily life? When, if ever, have you gone against these
ethical principles?

What patterns emerge in how you make ethical decisions? Do you feel
driven by a particular concept or idea?

Where do you go to find answers to life's most pressing questions? What
other ethical principles do you hold dear that you did not utilize in this
scenario?

Personal Space

This is your opportunity to add your own thoughts and make notes.

_____
_____
_____
_____
_____
_____
_____
_____
_____
_____
_____
_____
_____
_____

ACTIVITY PURPOSE

ACTIVITY PURPOSE

To organize the important events in your life that established your core spiritual beliefs. ◼

> " Our scientific power has outrun our spiritual power. We have guided missiles and misguided men."
>
> —*MARTIN LUTHER KING, JR.*

activity 2 **SPIRITUAL LIFELINES**

Like most of elements of your identity, there are parts of your spiritual identity that you are born with, and other parts you acquire through life experiences. It is these ethical, religious, or spiritual events that are the focus of this activity. You will explore these key events, dissect your memories, and analyze how these events have impacted your sense of spirituality. How do these events impact your actions now? Has your sense of spirituality changed over time? If so, how and why?

THE STEP BY STEP

1 You will begin by answering some very difficult spiritual questions. If you are stuck or struggling, feel free to skip and return to the more challenging items later. The initial questions are designed to directly address some of your core beliefs. The later questions are designed to get you thinking historically about your spirituality. When you answer any of the questions, think from the perspective of your spiritual, ethical, religious, and core beliefs.

What is your origin? Other than your mother/father, what gave you life? In other words, do you have beliefs about how you came to be and, if so, what are they?

_____

_____

_____

_____

Why are you here? What is your purpose? Do you believe your life has a preestablished meaning? Why or why not? When did you realize your greater calling (if that fits your perspective)?

_____

_____

_____

_____

What are the most important spiritual experiences that you can have in life? At what times do you believe they should occur? Which of them have already occurred and when did they happen?

_____

_____

_____

_____

_____

What will happen to you when you die? What is your belief
in the afterlife? At what age did you first realize this?

_____

_____

_____

_____

_____

When did you first realize your spirituality? What were the
circumstances that helped you to realize it?

_____

_____

_____

_____

_____

When did you first realize what ethics were? Who taught
you about them? Was there a specific incident that made
you realize that your inner being was guided by your
ethics?

_____

_____

_____

_____

_____

When has your spirituality been challenged the most? How
was it challenged and what did you learn about yourself
from that experience?

_____

_____

_____

_____

_____

At what points did your ethics/spirituality grow the most? How would you describe that growth? Was it a ceremony? Was it a personal meditative experience?

_____

_____

_____

_____

_____

" ——————————
The personal life deeply lived always expands into truths beyond itself."

—ANAIS NIN

——————————————

What were the most important moments in your life when you questioned why you are here, what is your purpose, and/or what will happen to you when you die? You most likely have more than one experience that fits this question; answer for each experience.

_____

_____

_____

_____

_____

2 Figure 8–2 illustrates a lifeline. Begin with your birth and list all of the major lessons and experiences that you have encountered over the years that have led to core spiritual beliefs. Some you may have remembered while answering the earlier questions; others might just pop into your mind (these have just as much merit!). As with a timeline, mark down the date (as close as you can remember) on your lifeline. Let yourself be free to brainstorm and add items that come to you.

3 Who was there to witness these ethical/spiritual events? Ask these individuals to review your lifeline and talk to them about your experiences. Ask them to describe their perspective of these events. What changes did they see you go through?

_____

_____

_____

_____

_____

_____

_____

SPIRITUAL LIFELINE

BIRTH

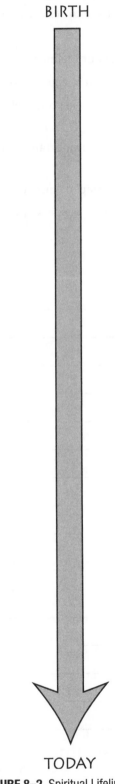

TODAY

FIGURE 8–2 Spiritual Lifeline

Reflections

Now that you have created a detailed chronology and history of your spiritual being, take some time to reflect on your lifeline using the following questions:

How do the events on your lifeline impact your actions now?

Has your sense of spirituality changed over time? If so, how and why?

What themes do you notice in your lifeline? Are there any consistent patterns?

What was the single, most important event in your lifeline and how has it impacted your life since?

How have these events shaped your current core spiritual beliefs?

What parts of your lifeline were easy to remember? Hard to remember? Why?

Personal Space

_____

_____

_____

_____

_____

_____

_____

_____

_____

_____

_____

_____

_____

_____

_____

activity 3 SPIRITUAL/ETHICAL/RELIGIOUS ROLE MODELS

You are not alone in developing your ethical/spiritual self. You have had role models who have helped to clarify and direct your beliefs. These important people play a fundamental role in shaping who you are. Spiritual, ethical, or religious leaders are not hard to find. Look beyond the obvious and/or the famous; sometimes our role models are family members, friends, and/or community members. Who inspires you? You will examine your relationships with these individuals and pick apart the lessons they shared with you to make meaning of your unique spiritual identity.

THE STEP BY STEP

1. In Figure 8–3, list your top five spiritual/ethical/religious role models, and determine why you chose them.

2. Think about each individual role model and consider the beliefs and actions that draw you toward them.

3. Describe a particular event or action of spiritual significance that each of your role models was involved with that empowered you to emulate that behavior. What were you thinking as you witnessed this event? How did this person act or react? What did you learn from it? Write down the event and its significance in Figure 8–4.

4. This is the best part of this activity. Seek out the people who you have listed as your spiritual/ethical/religious role models and tell them about the meaning that they hold in your life. If they are no longer with you or not reachable, think of how empowering and respectful it would be if you could talk to them.

ACTIVITY PURPOSE

To identify the individuals in your life who play(ed) the most significant role in shaping your spiritual identity. ◼

> I finally realized that being a role model doesn't mean people are encouraged to be like me—they're encouraged to go out and be more of themselves."
>
> —*LUCY LAWLESS*

Spiritual/Religious/Ethical Role Models	
Name	Beliefs, actions, and values that caused you to choose this person as a spiritual role model.

FIGURE 8–3

Top Five Spiritual/Ethical/Religious Role Models

SIGNIFICANT EVENT	WHAT DID YOU LEARN FROM THIS EVENT?

FIGURE 8–4
Significant Events with Role Models

Reflections

Thinking so closely about the people who have served as your most intimate role models is heartwarming. Actually telling them how you feel helps you to better realize the impact that they have on you.

Why did you choose these specific five role models?

What aspect of their spirituality do you admire the most?

What are the cornerstones of each role model's core beliefs that appeal to you?

What types of themes make up their personal code of ethics?

How do your role models go about living and teaching their values?

Can you think of situations where they taught you a lesson through their actions?

Personal Space

_____

_____

_____

_____

_____

_____

_____

_____

_____

_____

_____

_____

_____

_____

_____

_____

_____

_____

activity 4 **WHAT IS GOOD IN YOUR LIFE?**

Blessings, karma, goodwill, or *luck* are all terms for something good in your life. These moments are deeply connected to your spiritual being. Take a moment to think about what is good in your life.

As you think of these things, recognize how they create faith for you. Intentionally there is little in this chapter about how faith fits in to spiritual identity. "Faith" is often connected with established and traditional religions. This activity refers to faith in a different context, that of blessings or good things in your life. Blessings or good things in life give you faith and the belief that life is good. This positive flow of energy is what this activity is designed to ignite.

THE STEP BY STEP

1 In Figure 8–5, list your blessings under each of the categories. Do not worry about whether you are placing the right blessing into the right space. That is not important. What is important is that you write down as many as you possibly can.

Example

> Home: Caring for children.
>
> School/Work: Interesting and challenging work.
>
> Friends/Family: Watch my back.
>
> You/Society: Food is plentiful.

2 After you complete your list, highlight the five blessings that you depend on the most and write them down in Figure 8–6. What are your most sacred blessings? Which are the things that help you to retain the belief that good things will happen in your future?

3 For each of your five most sacred blessings, take some time to consider with whom you connect each of these blessings. Also consider the spiritual impact that these people have on your daily life.

Example

> Sacred Blessing
> I have a caring and loving family.
>
> Who in your life relates to these blessings?
> My children and partner, as well as my parents and extended family.
>
> What is the spiritual impact of these blessings?
> Because I know that my family is loving and supportive, I have feelings of peace and security.

4 Find a way to remind yourself daily of the core blessings and people whom you have discovered as a result of this activity.

ACTIVITY PURPOSE

To list and explore those things that are good in your life. ■

" Believe in yourself! Have faith in your abilities! Without a humble but reasonable confidence in your own powers you cannot be successful or happy."

—*NORMAN VINCENT PEALE*

What Are Your Blessings?

HOME	SCHOOL/WORK	FRIENDS/FAMILY	YOU/SOCIETY

FIGURE 8–5 What Are Your Blessings?

SACRED BLESSINGS	WHO IN YOUR LIFE RELATES TO THESE BLESSINGS?	WHAT IS THE SPIRITUAL IMPACT OF THESE BLESSINGS?
1.		
2.		
3.		
4.		
5.		

FIGURE 8–6 Connecting Your Blessings

Reflections

Now that you have extensively listed your blessings, it is time to connect them to how they define your spiritual identity.

In which areas of your life was it most difficult to think of good things? Why?

In what areas of your life was it easiest to think of good things? What do you think made it easy to come up with blessings in this area?

How often do you make a list of the good things in life? If you have never tried this before, why not?

What could you do differently to create more good in the world and thus for yourself?

Personal Space

_____

_____

_____

_____

_____

_____

_____

_____

_____

_____

_____

_____

_____

_____

_____

ACTIVITY PURPOSE

To create a religious/spiritual coat of arms that will represent your spiritual identity. ◼

" ————————
The family is changing, not disappearing. We have to broaden our understanding of it, look for the new metaphors."

—*MARY CATHERINE BATESON*

 activity 5 **SPIRITUAL COAT OF ARMS**

In the broadest sense, religion is a set of beliefs, values, and practices based on the teachings of a spiritual leader. This definition leaves room for a variety of faiths that may or may not be publicly recognized. This activity is designed to help you create a pictorial representation of your spiritual beliefs in the form of a coat of arms.

A "coat of arms" is a symbol of family heritage and nobility dating back to the eleventh century A.D. in Europe. Knights wore shields, ornately designed with their family crest, at public events to signify their family's values and nobility. Each crest was uniquely decorated with symbols that represented the family's code of honor. Knights wore their coat of armor proudly and used the symbolism to pass along important messages about what the family stood for from generation to generation.

You will create your own spiritual coat of arms to depict your spiritual core beliefs. Core beliefs are your perspective on what is your origin, purpose, meaning, and place in the world. These beliefs can be about how you relate with others, think about yourself, or view the world. Many times your core beliefs are rooted in religion. Your coat of arms can be used to symbolize what is most important to you based on your spiritual and religious values.

THE STEP BY STEP

1 *Blazon a name for your core beliefs.* First, begin with understanding how your religious/nonreligious beliefs fit into the world. The 22 largest organized religions globally are listed next. The population of secular, agnostic, nonreligious, and atheists is included, which makes up approximately 850 million people globally, the fourth largest group in the world. As you review this list, begin with the broadest sense of your faith. If you are struggling here, it may be helpful to review a source that lists thousands of organized religions globally (www.adherents.com).

1. Christianity: 2 billion

2. Islam: 1.3 billion

3. Hinduism: 900 million

4. Secular/nonreligious/agnostic/atheist: 850 million

5. Buddhism: 360 million

6. Chinese traditional religion: 225 million

7. Primal-indigenous: 150 million

8. African traditional and diasporic: 95 million

9. Sikhism: 23 million

10. Juche: 19 million

11. Spiritism: 14 million

12. Judaism: 14 million

13. Baha'i: 6 million

14. Jainism: 4 million

15. Shinto: 4 million

16. Cao Dai: 3 million

17. Tenrikyo: 2.4 million

18. Neo-Paganism: 1 million

19. Unitarian-universalism: 800 thousand

20. Rastafarianism: 700 thousand

21. Scientology: 600 thousand

22. Zoroastrianism: 150 thousand

What is the name for your religious beliefs?

_____

Using Figure 8–7, narrow the definition of your faith one step further. Most religions have derivations of how to practice the faith. These differences of practices are significant in some cases and are given a specific name. For example, Christianity is the largest faith in the United States (76 percent of the population); 52 percent of all Christians are Protestant, 24 percent are Catholic. Drilling down even further, the largest denomination of Protestants is Baptists. The largest Baptist population is Southern Baptists.

Can you break down the name of your faith further? Go as far as you can. The final name you come up with will be the name you put on the top of your spiritual coat of armor. Do not feel left out if your particular belief system does not "break down" this way. The goal of this step is to create the best heading for your spiritual coat of armor (Figure 8–8), not to get bogged down in the process.

2 *Create symbols for the primary tenets of your core beliefs.* Most faiths are built on a set of core beliefs about the origin, purpose, and meaning of life. If you do not follow a particular established faith, establish your own core beliefs. Answer the following questions to analyze your faith. Create symbols to add to your spiritual coat of arms (Figure 8–8) representing what is most important to you.

What is most important in your faith/core beliefs? What are the primary tenets of your faith/core beliefs? (Add your symbols to the upper left quadrant of your coat of armor.)

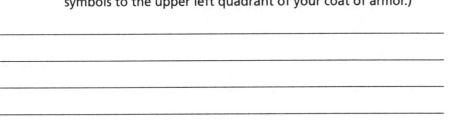

_____

_____

_____

_____

_____

_____

_____

_____

Who/what is the source of your spiritual core beliefs? (Add your symbols to the bottom left quadrant of your coat of armor.)

_____

_____

_____

_____

_____

_____

_____

_____

_____

_____

_____

What do you believe about how you should interact with other people, plants, animals, or other life forms? How do you interact with nature? (Add your symbols to the lower right quadrant of your coat of armor.)

_____

_____

_____

_____

_____

_____
_____
_____
_____
_____
_____
_____
_____

How do you practice your faith/core beliefs? (Add your symbols to the upper right quadrant of your spiritual coat of armor.)

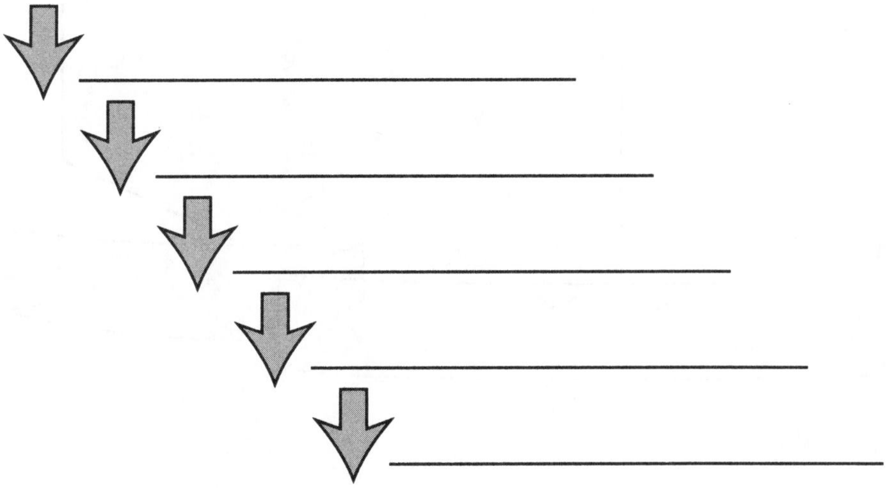

_____
_____
_____
_____
_____
_____
_____
_____
_____
_____
_____
_____
_____
_____

FIGURE 8–7
Naming Your Faith

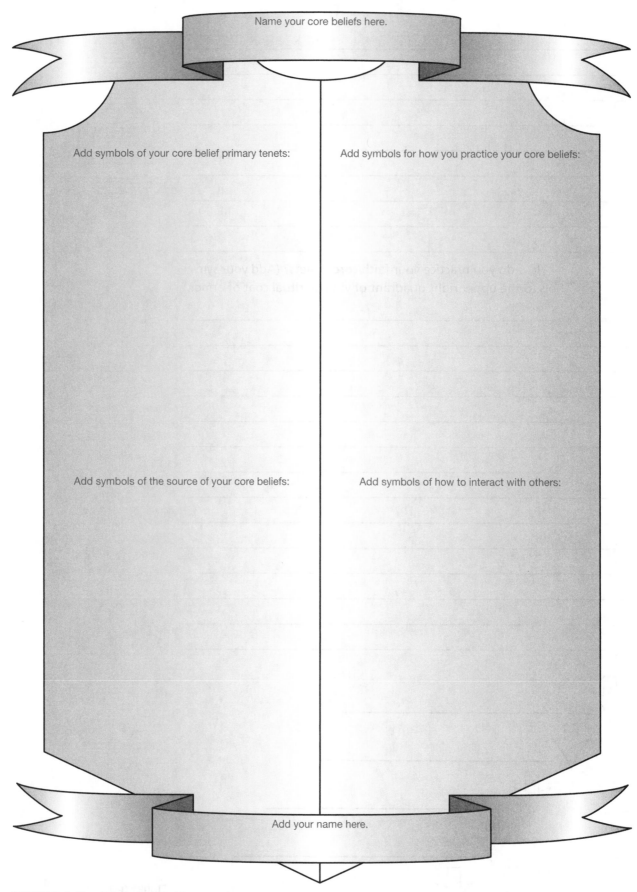

Name your core beliefs here.

Add symbols of your core belief primary tenets:

Add symbols for how you practice your core beliefs:

Add symbols of the source of your core beliefs:

Add symbols of how to interact with others:

Add your name here.

FIGURE 8–8 Your Spiritual Coat of Arms

Reflections

Coats of arms are designed to pass along important messages from generation to generation through symbolism.

Based on what you depicted on your coat of arms, what key messages do you wish to portray for future generations?

What core beliefs are most important to you spiritually?

When thinking about core beliefs, what was most difficult for you to convey in symbols? What made this message so difficult? If it is easier to express the message in words, please do so.

When have you used these core beliefs to make important decisions in your life? How do they help you to define who you are as a person?

Personal Space

_____

_____

_____

_____

_____

_____

_____

_____

_____

_____

_____

_____

_____

_____

_____

SPIRITUAL IDENTITY PERSONAL VISION PYRAMID

It is time now to make meaning out of the activities you have just completed. Using the Vision Pyramid, you will channel the energy within you to learn about your true identity.

1 What Is My Spiritual Identity?

As you progressed through the activities in this chapter, you no doubt began to notice consistent themes and ideas. Look through these activities and find 10 words, phrases, and ideas that are regularly occurring themes throughout your activity notes. Translate these themes into short statements to describe your spiritual identity. It is important to avoid making judgments at this point; they apply to core values in the following step. Simply pull out the observed themes. Write these 10 themes/statements here:

Example: *I believe that my source of spirituality is through my connection with and respect for nature.*

1. _____
2. _____
3. _____
4. _____
5. _____
6. _____
7. _____
8. _____
9. _____
10. _____

2 Develop Spiritual Core Values

Beginning with a solid sense of your identity is essential for developing meaningful core values. Core values are the principles, standards, or qualities that you consider worthwhile or desirable. Personal values form the criterion for evaluating what is important in your life. Look at the words, phrases, and ideas you listed in your core value statements. Look for specific themes. Do any of the themes merge? Spend some time looking at the 10 statements and find the patterns within. Condense the 10 words, phrases, and ideas listed above into five core values that fit how you feel you should live your life. Utilize the values list from Chapter 3 to help in the creation of this list. Write the five spiritual core values that you create here:

Example: *I believe in the balance of life through the yin/yang.*

1. _____
2. _____
3. _____
4. _____
5. _____

3 Create Specific Personal Spiritual Goals

Now it is time to create an action plan for your values! Creating effective personal goals fills the gap between who you are now and who you want to be. Review the core values that you have created and challenge yourself to develop specific actions (goals) for each one. What changes need to be made in your life to live by your core values? Remember, the best goals are S.M.A.R.T. (Specific, Measurable, Achievable, Realistic, and Timely). Begin by writing one personal goal for each core value here (you may wish to create more):

Example: *I will further research two works of Islam by studying the language that they were written in by the end of the summer.*

1. _____
2. _____
3. _____
4. _____
5. _____

4 Summarize Your Identity Area into a Spiritual Identity Mission Statement

Your identity, five core values, and personal goals are the building blocks for a successful identity area mission statement. Mission statements provide a synopsis of the strategy behind a set of individual goals; they are a short written description of your purpose and direction. Missions should be easy to remember and clarify where you want to go in life. In the personal space provided next, try to create a mission statement that summarizes your identity, values, and goals. Remember, mission statements are as unique as the individual creating them, and they don't need to be perfect!

Personal Space (My Spiritual Mission)

_____
_____
_____
_____
_____
_____
_____

_____

_____

_____

_____

_____

_____

_____

SPIRITUAL IDENTITY ALTERNATIVE ROUTES

The activities offered in this chapter should serve as an effective starting point for learning more about your spiritual identity. The following sections provide numerous other resources and ideas that we would like to point you toward as you continue to explore who you are.

VISIT A SPIRITUAL LEADER

If you have a priest, rabbi, minister, reverend, and so on, take some time to sit down with this person to gain a deeper understanding of your faith. Spiritual leaders can help you to solve spiritual dilemmas and can help you connect your personal spiritual values to your faith. Another avenue for discovery would be to read about spiritual leaders within your faith.

**For additional Web resources,
try searching with the following terms:**

Great spiritual leaders

Religious leaders

Saints

Clergy

FIND A NEW POINT OF VIEW

There are countless religions, philosophies, and faiths out there. If you are settled with your faith, your desire to develop spiritual identity will connect and strengthen what you already believe. If you are seeking new perspectives, developing your spiritual identity will include understanding and comparing many faiths. Because theoretically there are potentially as many faiths as there are people, it will help to begin by talking with people that you know about their faiths. Meeting with clergy from a variety of faiths can also give you new insight. Finally, countless books are available that describe, compare, and contrast the beliefs of the world.

**For additional Web resources,
try searching with the following terms:**

Faiths

Religion

Adherents

Spiritual belief systems

A SEARCH FOR SPIRIT

The *inner you,* the *soul,* the *life force*—many words and phrases bring to bear the idea of an internal energy source such as *chi* that keeps us alive. While many do not believe in such a concept, the idea of an energy field that binds together our consciousness is accepted by most. So what do you believe? How do you describe the inner source of life that you possess? Meditation can bring you great insight as to your life force, as can intentional spiritual experiences. Seek out opportunities that help you to understand the inner being that you possess.

**For additional Web resources,
try searching with the following terms:**

Chi energy

Soul

Life force

Personal spirit

Creating Your Personal Vision: The Journey

SUCCESS IS A JOURNEY, NOT A DESTINATION. THE DOING IS OFTEN

MORE IMPORTANT THAN THE OUTCOME.

■

—ARTHUR ASHE

DREAM LOFTY DREAMS, AND AS YOU DREAM, SO SHALL YOU BECOME.

YOUR VISION IS THE PROMISE OF WHAT YOU SHALL ONE DAY BE;

YOUR IDEAL IS THE PROPHECY OF WHAT YOU SHALL AT LAST UNVEIL.

■

—JAMES ALLEN

The symbol used to represent your personal journey is the symbol for infinity. Infinity comes from the Latin word *infinito*, which means "unending," and was created by mathematician John Wallis in the late 1600s. This symbol is very fitting in that it represents not only an unending process, but also the idea that on your personal journey, you will have countless experiences that will shape who you are. It is the combination of all of these numerous experiences that shapes the unique journey of your personal development.

Congratulations on making it this far! Your time and efforts are no doubt bringing you clarity and understanding about what makes you such a unique person. This chapter is where you pull together all of your hard work.

Your personal vision is a representation of your philosophy, life calling, or purpose. It encompasses all of your mission statements, core values, and goals. It is a symbolic message or gesture that is simple for you to understand and should be easy for you to picture and/or remember.

Your personal vision can be in whatever format makes the most sense to you; there are fewer rules than opportunities to express yourself. A personal vision does not have to be written in a specified manner or even written at all (although it is very common to do so). Artwork can capture your personal vision. Music can capture your personal vision. Poetry, lists, collages, crafts, recordings, videos—all of these can be used to capture or reflect your personal vision. For the purposes of this book, you may wish to begin with a written expression of vision, since many of the activities in this workbook have been focused on written reflection. You may find over time that your personal vision becomes more like an entity or mantra than a written statement.

YOUR PERSONAL VISION CAN BE IN WHATEVER FORMAT MAKES

THE MOST SENSE TO YOU.

The most important guideline for vision creation is that your expression of personal vision should hold a clear and concise meaning for you. This meaning should be consistently applicable to any and every area of your life. When faced with a difficult decision, you should be able to summon your personal vision for guidance. Equally, in the moments that make up the everyday, your personal vision will help you to create consistency and purpose in life. Now you will begin to select the most important experiences from your life journey to create your personal vision.

Once you begin crafting your vision, don't let your frustrations with the creative process tempt you to give up. This book is about the process of personal discovery and the journey, not just a product of personal vision. Your vision is the proverbial icing on the cake. As you grow and evolve personally, so too will your personal vision evolve and keep you growing. Look for opportunities to incorporate something new into your vision and allow it to guide your own evolution. Keep in mind the symbol for the journey, which encompasses endless experience and unending growth.

THIS BOOK IS ABOUT THE PROCESS OF PERSONAL DISCOVERY AND THE JOURNEY,

NOT JUST A PRODUCT OF PERSONAL VISION.

THE TEMPTATION TO "BE DONE"

One of the most difficult ideas that we have presented is that the visioning process is just that, a process. This means that you may never be done with this creative journey. You may find that your core values shift as you progress in your life and, most certainly, your goals will change. None of the ideas presented in this book are static. The creative process that you use to bring your life passion into positive use will shift as you continue to accumulate experiences on your life's journey. To consider your journey complete after creating your first personal vision is to discount the experiences that will occur in your future.

There is a natural need within most people to complete a task or to find closure to a process in order to feel a sense of accomplishment. Many people need that feeling of accomplishment in order to stay energized and continue getting things done. No doubt, you have accomplished a great many things so far in this book. Think of the goals that you have set, the core values that you have determined, and the changes that you have already made to your life! The creation of your personal vision is not the last accomplishment in this process.

> It is good to have an end to journey towards; but it is the journey that matters in the end."
>
> —URSULA K. LeGUIN

Your need for completion is respectable. However, be aware of some of the drawbacks that come with focusing solely on completion. When you are constantly focused on your desire to finish a task, you may well be missing out on some important life lessons. These may be discoveries about yourself, those around you, or the task itself.

To apply an analogy, imagine quickly climbing a ladder to get to the top. The harder you work to get to the top, the less likely you are to notice the wall that you are climbing. Is the ladder stable? Are you able to notice other tasks of importance on your way up the ladder? The ladder may even be leaning against the wrong wall. Speed is only as beneficial as its purpose and direction. Being aware and appreciative of the journey may give you some important clues to your direction. Before you have to go all the way back down the ladder, stop and think about whether you are metaphorically climbing the right wall!

GOING NOWHERE FAST

Have you ever heard the adage "People who are always focused on getting things done and moving on often find themselves staying put"? What typically follows when you get something "done"? Do you pack up and move on to something else? Why work so hard and so fast to get somewhere if you don't know where you are going? Pay attention to the processes in your life that lead you to completing a task; it is through this understanding that you gain better knowledge of how you personally experience success.

PEOPLE WHO ARE ALWAYS FOCUSED ON GETTING THINGS DONE AND MOVING

ON OFTEN FIND THEMSELVES STAYING PUT.

It is a bit ironic that so many cultures place such a premium on task completion. The Internet age is quickening our pace and sometimes deadening our perceptions. We compute hundreds of decisions per hour with information streaming through our beings at continually increasing speeds. We filter through a myriad of data endlessly only to make a quick decision and then move to the next nano-task. Does one more decision make you happier or does it lead to more questions and then more decisions? This endless factoring and decision making forces you to quicken your pace but does not always lead you in the right direction. You climb endless ladders, but you do not process why you did so or even determine if you answered the question at a depth that produces a truly useful solution.

Multitasking is an absolute necessity. Can you simultaneously e-mail, chat, speak with someone on the phone, and flip through papers without missing a beat? When those tasks are done, do you move on to another call, another e-mail, and another shuffle? In a typical moment, how many of the tasks shown in Figure 9–1 do you feel you can complete at the same time? (Check all that apply.)

Now consider, how many of these things are you doing to the best of your abilities? How many of the ladders that you have placed before you to climb are you climbing with intention and care?

____	E-mail
____	Instant messaging
____	Talk on phone
____	Listen to music/watch TV
____	Doodle
____	Other: ________________

FIGURE 9–1
Multitasking

"Continual improvement is an unending journey."

—*LLOYD DOBENS AND CLARE CRAWFORD-MASON*

The personal vision process requires skills other than multitasking. The skill you need the most at this point is *focus*. Turn off your cell phone, put away your iPod, and close out of your e-mail, instant messenger, and Internet browser. Now turn on your mind, heart, spirit, and body to new discovery. This is not a race to a finish line. This process is about looking around to see if you are climbing the right wall. It asks you to slow down a bit, really dig into yourself, and be in tune with your values. Take some time to find some privacy because what you are about to do is deeply personal. This is an opportunity to literally resynchronize your life. It is a chance to study your personal journey and better shape the place you are about to go!

In the following personal space, jot down a few thoughts about your state of mind in this visioning journey. What have you learned about yourself? What has been difficult in this process? What are some goals that you have already accomplished? Do you see the need to focus on the process of creating your personal vision, or are you more focused on just "getting done"?

Personal Space

This is your opportunity to add your own thoughts and make notes.

_____

_____

_____

_____

GATHER YOUR VITAL VISIONING INFORMATION

The first step in creating a personal vision is to flip back through this book and write down some vital information about your values, goals, and mission statements from each of the five elements of identity chapters (Chapters 4 through 8). Doing this will help you to connect the themes that you have uncovered during your journey!

You will recall that you created mission statements and core values for each of the five identity elements. On the following few pages, write down these vital pieces of information. By bringing together the missions and values that you have created, you will begin to notice themes emerging that will help you to understand what your overall core values and personal vision are.

COGNITIVE IDENTITY ELEMENT
MY COGNITIVE IDENTITY MISSION STATEMENT AND VALUES

Write your cognitive identity mission statement here and record your cognitive core values in Figure 9–2. You can find your cognitive mission statement and core values on pages 69–71.

_____

_____

_____

_____

_____

COGNITIVE IDENTITY

is your personal perspective of the achievements, improvements, and exercise of your mind.

Cognitive Core Values

1. _____

2. _____

3. _____

4. _____

5. _____

FIGURE 9–2
My Cognitive Core Values

Discuss one experience that you had while exploring your cognitive identity that had a great impact on you:

_____

_____

_____

_____

_____

How strongly do you connect with your cognitive identity? How much do you think your cognitive identity will shape your overall personal vision? How important is your cognitive identity in determining who you are? Why?

_____

_____

_____

_____

_____

CULTURAL IDENTITY

is your personal perspective of society, culture, and personal relationships.

CULTURAL IDENTITY ELEMENT
MY CULTURAL IDENTITY MISSION STATEMENT AND VALUES

Write your cultural identity mission statement here and record your cultural core values in Figure 9–3. You can find your cultural mission statement and core values on pages 95–97.

_____

_____

_____

_____

_____

FIGURE 9–3
My Cultural Core Values

Cultural Core Values

1. _____

2. _____

3. _____

4. _____

5. _____

Discuss one experience that you had while exploring your cultural identity that had a great impact on you:

_____
_____
_____
_____
_____

How strongly do you connect with your cultural identity? How much do you think your cultural identity will shape your overall personal vision? How important is your cultural identity in determining who you are? Why?

_____
_____
_____
_____
_____

EMOTIONAL IDENTITY ELEMENT
MY EMOTIONAL IDENTITY MISSION STATEMENT AND VALUES

Write your emotional identity mission statement here and record your emotional core values in Figure 9–4. You can find your emotional mission statement and core values on pages 127–129.

_____
_____
_____
_____
_____

EMOTIONAL IDENTITY

is your personal perspective of how your feelings guide who you are and how you see the world.

Emotional Core Values

1. _____
2. _____
3. _____
4. _____
5. _____

FIGURE 9–4
My Emotional Core Values

Discuss one experience that you had while exploring your emotional identity that had a great impact on you:

_____

_____

_____

_____

_____

How strongly do you connect with your emotional identity? How much do you think your emotional identity will shape your overall personal vision? How important is your emotional identity in determining who you are? Why?

_____

_____

_____

_____

_____

PHYSICAL IDENTITY

is your personal perspective of how you value your body.

PHYSICAL IDENTITY ELEMENT
MY PHYSICAL IDENTITY MISSION STATEMENT AND VALUES

Write your physical identity mission statement here and record your physical core values in Figure 9–5. You can find your physical mission statement and core values on pages 151–153.

_____

_____

_____

_____

_____

FIGURE 9–5
My Physical Core Values

Physical Core Values
1. _____
2. _____
3. _____
4. _____
5. _____

Discuss one experience that you had while exploring your physical identity that had a great impact on you:

_____

_____

_____

_____

_____

How strongly do you connect with your physical identity? How much do you think your physical identity will shape your overall personal vision? How important is your physical identity in determining who you are? Why?

_____

_____

_____

_____

_____

_____

SPIRITUAL IDENTITY ELEMENT
MY SPIRITUAL IDENTITY MISSION STATEMENT AND VALUES

Write your spiritual identity mission statement here and record your spiritual core values in Figure 9–6. You can find your spiritual mission statement and core values on pages 179–181.

_____

_____

_____

_____

_____

SPIRITUAL IDENTITY

is your personal perspective of your religious, ethical, and/or sacred beliefs.

Spiritual Core Values

1. _____

2. _____

3. _____

4. _____

5. _____

FIGURE 9–6
My Spiritual Core Values

Discuss one experience that you had while exploring your spiritual identity that had a great impact on you:

_____

_____

_____

_____

_____

How strongly do you connect with your spiritual identity? How much do you think your spiritual identity will shape your overall personal vision? How important is your spiritual identity in determining who you are? Why?

_____

_____

_____

_____

_____

THE PERSONAL VISION WORKSHEET

The key to creating a personal vision is to narrow down the core values that you developed for all of the five elements of identity. Begin by listing in Figure 9–7 any core values that occur in more than one of your five elements of identity and list how many times you utilized that value. (You may have fewer than 10—that is okay.)

VALUE	NUMBER OF TIMES USED
1.	
2.	
3.	
4.	
5.	
6.	
7.	
8.	
9.	
10.	

FIGURE 9–7
Core Value Discovery

You have successfully analyzed your identity in order to identify its building blocks. Now you are bringing all of those blocks together in a meaningful way to symbolize the whole of your identity. The values listed in Figure 9–7 should feel sacred to you. They are the core of who you are!

YOUR FIVE CORE VALUES

In Figure 9–8, jot down the five key values, ideas, or phrases that you feel you need to include when creating a personal vision. You may need to combine some of the earlier core values (the ones from your identity areas) to fully connect to who you are. Remember, to an extent, these five core values are symbolic representations of your entire visioning process. Their meaning is much deeper than the letters or the words in them. They are a symbol of your journey, and only you can understand the depth of your core being.

When you have your five core values in place, they form the five most important ideas in your life. These ideas are the building blocks of your life.

Your Five Core Values

1. _____
2. _____
3. _____
4. _____
5. _____

FIGURE 9–8
Your Five Core Values

Reflections

Think of a major life decision you need to make and then answer the following questions:

Could you use these five core values as a guide for how you will proceed?

What parts of your personality, your personal history, or your identity are not represented by the five core values?

Would you be comfortable if someone close to you described you using your five core values?

How do the five core values that you have developed compare with the values you discovered in Chapter 3, using the value sorter activity?

Personal Space

_____
_____
_____
_____

_____

_____

_____

_____

_____

_____

_____

_____

_____

_____

CREATING YOUR PERSONAL VISION

Now that you discovered your five core values, you can use them to create your personal vision. The great thing about your core values is that they mean so much more to you now than just being five appealing values. You have invested a significant amount of time and effort in developing the meaning behind these values. They are now sacred to you.

SOME GUIDELINES FOR PERSONAL VISION CREATION

- Do not limit yourself and your creativity.

- If you create a written statement, make it memorable enough so that you can recite it with gusto!

- Do not complete this task in one sitting. Create a draft, put the book down, and come back and review. Remember—process, not product.

- As you are creating your vision, keep your list of primary values, themes, and ideas in front of you.

MINI ACTIVITIES TO BEGIN THE PERSONAL VISION CREATION PROCESS

Complete these short activities incorporating the list of your five core values. These activities are intended to unlock different parts of your brain so that your personal vision is as inclusive as possible.

1. Finish the following statement in five different ways in Figure 9–9, attributing each statement to one of your five core values:

    I believe that I am a person who . . .

CORE VALUE	STATEMENT

FIGURE 9–9
Core Values and Statements

2. In the following personal space, make a list or sketch of images that come to your mind when you think of each of your five core values.

3. In the following personal space, create a descriptive list of words that come to mind when you consider each of your five core values.

_____

_____

_____

_____

_____

_____

_____

_____

4. In Figure 9–10, write down each of your five core values and consider the following prompts: who, what, where, how, when, and why. In other words, test each of your core values by asking each of these questions.

CORE VALUE	WHO, WHAT, WHERE, HOW, WHEN, AND WHY
1.	
2.	
3.	
4.	
5.	

FIGURE 9–10
Test Your Core Values

MY PERSONAL VISION: DRAFT I

You have tested your five core values in numerous ways. It is time to create a representation of these values as your personal vision. Remember that this does not have to be a written statement, but putting your vision into words may serve as a good starting point. Now bring the core values into focus to create your personal vision in the following space:

_____

_____

_____

_____

_____

_____

_____

Once you've completed your first draft, stop! Take a break and come back to the process a bit later.

MY PERSONAL VISION: DRAFT 2

Now that you took a break, look again at your core values, themes, and ideas. Are there any changes that you would like to make to your initial expression of vision? How does your personal vision feel to you? Do you think it accurately depicts who you are and who you want to be? When you read it out loud, does it "pop" for you? Take some time to refine your personal vision if needed:

_____

_____

_____

_____

_____

_____

Continue the process of refining your personal vision until you reach a point where you believe the expression that you created is a fair, memorable, and authentic representation of who you are. This expression is intended to be a reminder of the entire process that you experienced in this book. Your personal vision is truly more than the sum of its parts, and it is something only you will ever fully know.

YOUR PERSONAL VISION IS TRULY MORE THAN THE SUM OF ITS PARTS,

AND IT IS SOMETHING ONLY YOU WILL EVER FULLY KNOW.

Remember, your personal vision should be a work in progress—forever. Keep your eyes open for opportunities to incorporate something new into your personal vision. Allow it to evolve as you use it to guide your own evolution.

Bring your new experiences into the process of revising your personal vision, but scrutinize your decisions. Chances are, when you've created the right vision for yourself, it will resonate in every aspect of your life. Only when something occurs in your life that truly shakes your foundation should you consider rethinking your personal vision. At that point, your mission statements will probably shift, and you may even think differently about your core values. The more you are able to consistently evaluate your life, the more congruent you will be with your deepest, driving beliefs.

Your opportunity to connect your discoveries more deeply and on a larger scale occurs in Chapter 10!

Being You, Sharing You!

Now that you have reached this point in your journey (remember that the process of applying and revising your vision is a journey, it is ongoing!), you may be thinking "What am I going to do with all of this new inspiration and direction?" Not to avoid the answer, but really it is up to you. This may be a life-changing experience that inspires you to take on new tasks and find new life direction. For others, it may have a more subtle impact, possibly a sense of renewed motivation.

In this chapter, we want to share with you how this workbook impacted others before you, and direct you in finding ways to take advantage of your new self-awareness. We also ask you to share what you learned with us by going online to http://www.myvisionportal.com!

www.myvisionportal.com

MYVISIONPORTAL.COM

This book is an exploration of YOU! From our perspective, this exploration is our professional passion. We have spent a great deal of our careers and personal lives trying to better understand what drives people. We believe that understanding these motivating experiences and values will help future generations of friends, family members, colleagues, life partners, counselors, clergy, supervisors, and so forth better understand each other.

As is evident in this book, the value of better understanding yourself is that it helps you to grow. That growth is constant and will continue to develop as you experience more of what life has to offer.

A CONGRUENT LIFE

The idea of living a congruent life is not a new idea. It is often referred to as "living with integrity." It is about living a life that is in support of, and guided by, your personal vision. It means that your decisions, actions, thoughts, and reactions should be generally demonstrating your vision. It also means that you will live life "tuned in" and fully aware of situations that are incongruent with your vision, and you will respond in ways that will realign you with your vision. By becoming more aware of how you live life, and learning how to rely on your vision, you'll find new motivation and purpose for your life.

Myvisionportal.com is an interactive source of vision statements, mission statements, and core values from which you can learn and be inspired. On the site, you can share your story and learn from others' journeys. By creating a resource of examples and inspiration, everyone involved will better understand what motivates and leads people to success.

BY CREATING A RESOURCE OF EXAMPLES AND INSPIRATION,

EVERYONE INVOLVED WILL BETTER UNDERSTAND WHAT MOTIVATES

AND LEADS PEOPLE TO SUCCESS.

WHAT WE LEARNED ABOUT VISIONING

Visioning is the process of learning about yourself by developing core values and identity areas and then creating goals, mission statements, and a personal vision. Basically, this workbook represents a framework for this process, but as you may have already realized by engaging with this book, the experience means much more than a couple hundred pages.

As was stated earlier, the process of visioning impacts people differently. Some have quite literally trudged their way through it . . . fighting it tooth and nail until the end, and then are surprised that they feel very little has changed. These people were probably trying to engage in this process at the wrong time in their lives—they were not truly invested in personal understanding and growth. (Or at least not invested in the method that we have prepared!)

VISIONING IS THE PROCESS OF LEARNING ABOUT YOURSELF BY DEVELOPING

YOUR CORE VALUES AND IDENTITY AREAS AND THEN CREATING GOALS, MISSION

STATEMENTS, AND A PERSONAL VISION.

For some, the experience is earth shattering; it causes people to take stock of their lives and evaluate the decisions they are making. There is a sense of deep realization and motivation to move forward in life, make use of newfound personal knowledge, and have a deeper understanding of their personal identity. These people were probably engaging in this process at the right time and place. These people were able to make the connection between our method and their development. (We hope this fits your experience!)

The most important thing, however, is that you are able to utilize whatever pieces resonated for you. Maybe there was a key exercise that really impacted you or maybe your vision turned into your interpersonal calling. Whatever the impact, please know that you are in pleasant company.

In Figures 10–1, 10–2, and 10–3, you will get to know a bit more about us, the three authors of this book. We feel like it is a bit unfair to ask you to share your personal story, core values, and personal vision without doing so ourselves. You will see that all three of us define ourselves differently, and that all three of our visions are formulated quite differently.

Name: Tobin Burgess

Age: 32	Sex: Male

Occupation: Human Resource Business Partner, Consultant, and Life Coach

Personal information (250 words about who you are . . . the content is your choice!).

Personally, I love to smile, laugh, tell stories, run, and explore nature. Currently I live in Seattle, Washington, with my loyal pup Caro. Friends and family that I love surround me. Helping people and organizations make good decisions to bring out their greatest potential is incredibly exciting for me. For this reason, my primary occupation is as a human resources professional for a large software development company with a similar mission. I also work as a consultant and coach through Evergreen3 Consulting. Spiritually I live with a personal relationship with God that knows no boundaries.

Primary Identity Area

Emotional Identity

Personal Mission Statements

Cognitive Mission Statement: Be a light, not a judge. Be a solution, not a problem. Live, learn, and teach others and myself to continually reach their greatest potential through experiential, academic, and explorative learning.

Cultural Mission Statement: Embrace my authentic Iowa, white, straight, Christian, educated heritage without guilt and full of pride and respect for all people and life forms.

Emotional Mission Statement: Love unconditionally all people and life forms by opening my heart, sharing my passion, and being real.

Physical Mission Statement: Treat my body and health, as well as others', as a gift from God.

Spiritual Mission Statement: Live life with passion, forgiveness, love, balance, and harmony with all God's creation. Intentionally cultivate, grow, and share positive energy and inspiration with all.

5 Core Values

1. **Unconditional Love**—Nurture and develop all life forms by consistently showing tough love especially when love is not requested but most needed.
2. **Abundant Inspiration**—Be a light, not a judge. Live life with passion and endless positive energy.
3. **Lifelong Learning**—Be a continuous learner and teacher to reach our fullest potential.
4. **Harmony**—Live a balanced life by loving God, environmental sustainability, and peace.
5. **Authenticity**—Love oneself and other completely, mind, body, spirit, heart, and relationships, for who they are and want to be.

Personal Vision

Live Naked.

Please don't be offended! I mean an emotional, spiritual, and natural sense of naked. This term is deeply personal to me. It is a bit racy and edgy, but not made to offend. The term comes from a song by the BoDeans that truly captures the passion and essence of being open, vulnerable, confident, and completely loving.

How *The Personal Vision Workbook* Has Impacted Your Life (250 words or less):

The genesis of this book came about in 1997 when I, like many other people, was going through a major transformation in my life. This is when I first discovered my vision, "Live Naked." Since then I've gone through many other upheavals and transformations, but one thing has remained quite constant: my vision. The picture/feeling/sense of who I am stuck with me and pulled me through the best of times and worst of times. I am incredibly excited to share this opportunity with you. It just works! May you be as blessed as I am with a clear authentic personal vision. Thank you for being you and letting me be naked.

FIGURE 10–1 Tobin Burgess's Vision

Name: Kevin Pugh

| Age: 35 | Sex: Male |

Occupation: I am fully occupied by LIFE!

Personal information (250 words about who you are . . . the content is your choice!).

I'm a brand-new DAD! It really is amazing what this did to my perspective on life. After a twelve-year career in Higher Education Administration and College Student Development, teaching and training others to discover and develop their identity, I now have a whole new part of my heart, mind, and body that has been "activated." Formerly a comfortable passenger of life, I am rediscovering the blessing it is to be here and to be an imperfect, evolving being. I am discovering new depths to my love in marriage, and new stability provided by my faith. I am discovering new capabilities of my body through marathons and triathlons. I am finding new ways to work for peace and social justice through a new job in Restorative Justice. I am rediscovering the passion I have for discovery itself. To this lifelong process I bring a belief that the journey is greater than the destination and that gifts lie hidden in conflict and challenge.

Primary Identity Area

Cultural Identity

Personal Mission Statements

Cognitive Mission Statement: I will learn for life.

Cultural Mission Statement: I will love and respect.

Emotional Mission Statement: I will set feelings free.

Physical Mission Statement: I will be well, to do good.

Spiritual Mission Statement: I will listen and give.

5 Core Values

1. Love
2. Learn
3. Lend
4. Live
5. Laugh

Personal Vision

Harmonizing head, heart, and hands.

To discover and fulfill my life calling requires a balance of thought, passion, and action. Head—to LEARN; heart—to LOVE; hands—to LEND. I will LIVE life as an active participant. I will LAUGH, enjoying life and maintaining perspective through my sense of humor.

How *The Personal Vision Workbook* Has Impacted Your Life (250 words or less):

Writing this book, and subsequently using it, has been a journey of discovery and exacerbation. It has highlighted my strengths and my shortcomings simultaneously and magnified them exponentially. I've started to view the idea of balance and harmony in new ways. Specifically, I've realized that my "ideal" balance is always changing. It is both a reliable foundation and a flowing river. It can be a solid support and a soft landing. It goes where it needs to go, becomes what it needs to be. It is shaped by external influences as much as it shapes and guides me.

FIGURE 10–2 Kevin Pugh's Vision

Name: Leo Sevigny

Age: 35	Sex: Male

Occupation: College Administrator, College Instructor, Consultant, Author

Personal information (250 words about who you are . . . the content is your choice!).

I have a beautiful wife, Heather, who reminds me that the world is a place without limits.

I am the father of two children, Whitney and Sebastien, who remind me every day that no day is ever the same . . . or boring!

I live in and am a native of the state of Vermont.

I believe it takes a village to raise a child.

I believe that all people have the deep desire to understand others and be understood.

I believe that balance is the key to life.

I believe in a peaceful existence, not only for myself, but for all people.

I believe in the power of opposites, and the ability for two forces to balance perfectly.

Primary Identity Area

Cognitive Identity

Personal Mission Statements

Cognitive Mission Statement: My curiosity and creativity invite me to innovate.

Cultural Mission Statement: We are all one from the same source.

Emotional Mission Statement: Be a part of the laughter and the peace.

Physical Mission Statement: I am at my best when my movements are without effort.

Spiritual Mission Statement: Be one with the Tao.

5 Core Values

1. Integrity
2. Innovation
3. Harmony
4. Respect
5. Peace

Personal Vision

Toes Should Be Free . . .

Nothing is more refreshing than toes uncovered, resting on a beach, funneling through the sand . . . or the same toes being rubbed by a loved one. The point is, they need to be free. I believe all people should be pampered and respected for who they are, not for what society tells them they should be. I should not have to cover up who I am. . . . I, and my toes, should be free.

How *The Personal Vision Workbook* Has Impacted Your Life (250 words or less):

This workbook has allowed me to bring to life a passion that has lived within me for many years. It has also been a process that has confirmed friendships with my coauthors that I hold very close to my heart. It has allowed me to better understand myself through the creative process. This book is a realization of a dream, and I believe it will help others to realize theirs.

FIGURE 10–3 Leo Sevigny's Vision

MAKING SELF-INFORMED DECISIONS IN EACH OF THE FIVE IDENTITY AREAS

Regardless of the life decision before you and which area of your identity it impacts most, certain boundaries and considerations can come to mind that will help you make good choices. You have internal mechanisms that weigh out the pros and cons and force you to take on different perspectives until you ultimately make a comfortable and effective choice.

Based on the five elements of identity, there are a variety of questions that you may consider while making decisions. Utilize the following questions to help guide your decisions in the future.

COGNITIVE IDENTITY (MIND)

How will your decision stimulate your intellectual curiosities?

How will your decision impact how you spend your mental energy?

How will your decision coincide with how you learn best?

How will your decision bring new knowledge into your life?

CULTURAL IDENTITY (RELATIONSHIPS)

How will your decision impact friends, family, and how you relate with others?

How will your decision find congruence with your cultural and familial beliefs?

How will your decision impact your lifestyle, where you live, and your home?

How will your decision impact with whom you spend your time?

EMOTIONAL IDENTITY (HEART)

How will your decision be swayed by the emotions that you feel in the situation?

How will your decision impact the perception others have about your emotional being?

How will your decision emotionally impact you over the near future, the distant future?

How will your decision challenge your emotional safety?

PHYSICAL IDENTITY (BODY)

How will your decision impact your personal health and fitness?

How will your decision affect the amount of stress you experience?

How will your decision change the time you spend relaxing and rejuvenating?

How will your decision impact what you eat and how you eat it?

Name: (optional)

Age:	Sex:

Occupation:

Personal information (250 words about who you are . . . the content is your choice!).

Primary Identity Area

Personal Mission Statements

Cognitive Mission Statement:

Cultural Mission Statement:

Emotional Mission Statement:

Physical Mission Statement:

Spiritual Mission Statement:

5 Core Values

1.

2.

3.

4.

5.

Personal Vision

How *The Personal Vision Workbook* Has Impacted Your Life (250 words or less):

FIGURE 10–4 Worksheet for Your Personal Vision

SPIRITUAL IDENTITY (SPIRIT)

How will your decision affect your spiritual beliefs and your sense of spiritual identity?

How will your decision impact your ability to practice your faith?

How will your decision be measured alongside the values of your spiritual beliefs?

How will your decision impact your spiritual integrity?

CONNECTING TO OTHERS

One of the most powerful aspects of creating personal vision is the deep self-awareness that results. It is natural for you to now wonder what other people discovered as they worked their way through this process. The best way to find that out is to discuss with other readers, face to face, what they learned and gained though this process. If you are engaging in vision creation as a part of a staff, a class, or a group of friends, the sharing potential is quite exciting.

If you wish to gain a broader insight into people's experiences throughout the world, you can do so by accessing Myvisionportal.com. You will need to create a username and password and will enter information into a worksheet about who you are, your personal values, goals, mission, and vision. The format will follow our three examples presented in the figures in this chapter. Utilize the form shown in Figure 10–4 to bring together the information that you will input into the Web page.

By reading about others, you will learn about the variety of processes people go through in creating their personal visions. You will better understand the variety and creativity that people use in creating their personal direction. You will also have access to additional activity ideas and resources for utilizing your personal vision in your personal, educational, and workplace settings, and Web links to additional resources.

We hope to see you online, where we can continue to assist you in your journey!